D1551127

REVISED & UPDATED

COACHING YOUTH
BASEBALL

THIRD EDITION

The Guide for Coaches, Parents and Athletes

John P. McCarthy, Jr.

FOREWORD BY JEFF MCKAY
MENTOR COACH, MAJOR LEAGUE BASEBALL

BETTERWAY BOOKS
Cincinnati, Ohio

11 10 09 08 07   5 4 3 2 1

Distributed in Canada by Fraser Direct, 100 Armstrong Avenue, Georgetown, ON, Canada L7G 5S4, Tel: (905) 877-4411. Distributed in the U.K. and Europe by David & Charles, Brunel House, Newton Abbot, Devon, TQ12 4PU, England, Tel: (+44) 1626 323200, Fax: (+44) 1626 323319, E-mail: postmaster@davidandcharles.co.uk. Distributed in Australia by Capricorn Link, P.O. Box 704, Windsor, NSW 2756 Australia, Tel: (02) 4577-3555.

Library of Congress Cataloging-in-Publication Data

McCarthy, John P., 1947-
  Coaching youth baseball : the guide for coaches, parents and athletes / By John P. McCarthy, Jr. -- 3rd ed.
      p. cm.
  Rev. ed. of: Youth baseball. c.1996.
  Includes bibliographical references and index.
  ISBN-13: 978-1-55870-793-1 (pbk. : alk. paper)
  ISBN-10: 1-55870-793-X
  1. Baseball for children--Coaching. 2. Youth league baseball--Coaching. I. Title.

GV880.4.M33 2007
796.35707'7--dc22   2006027505

Edited by Michelle Ehrhard
Designed by Grace Ring
Illustrations by John Rizzo
Cover design by Sean Braemer and Claudean Wheeler
Cover photography by Christine Polomsky
Page layout by Eric West
Production coordinated by Mark Griffin

ABOUT THE AUTHOR

Jack McCarthy, like many Americans, is a sports enthusiast and has played and coached numerous sports all of his life. As a parent, and now grandparent, he knows that athletic competition builds self-confidence in young people. It also prepares them to handle life's challenges and teaches them how to succeed. The Betterway Coaching Kids series was developed by Jack to help parents and coaches ensure that their child's experience in sports is a positive one.

Jack is an attorney and works for the New Jersey Courts. He lives with his wife and family, which includes three children and four grandchildren, in Hillsborough, New Jersey. His other books in the series include titles on soccer, basketball, and football. He has also written *Baseball's All-Time Dream Team*.

DEDICATION

To my wife, my best friend, my life coach, Linda Jo.
Thanks, Smiley.

ACKNOWLEDGMENTS

Special thanks to my photo models:
East Brunswick all-star Connor McCarthy, also Chris Goggins, Joe McCarthy, Chris and Scott Demarest, Lauren and Patrick McCann, and Joe and Jamie Capodiferro.

TABLE OF CONTENTS

FOREWORD

By Jeff McKay, Mentor Coach, Major League Baseball, St. Louis Cardinals, San Francisco Giants; Director, Be Your Own Coach; Mentor Trainer, Positive Coaching Alliance; Visiting Coach, Middlebury College

If you're a parent/coach I'll bet you face the same challenge I do—getting your child/player to pay attention. Maybe he listens while you are teaching, but loses what you said when you move on. Or maybe he can keep it together in practice, but falls apart in a game. Sound familiar? There are ways to meet this challenge.

In this book, John McCarthy, Jr., offers many effective methods for coaching kids. His ideas on how to run practices and motivate players will help you gain and keep your players' attention. With the guidance of some creative mentors, and through the school of hard knocks, I've also discovered a way to get kids to learn so they can *retain* what they've learned without direct supervision, and most importantly, in the "cauldron of competition." It's an approach I call Be Your Own Coach. I offer it as further food for thought to be used in conjunction with what McCarthy says about coaching youth baseball.

As head coach of Be Your Own Coach, a mentor trainer for the Positive Coaching Alliance, and a Super Coach for Major League Baseball, I conduct clinics for coaches of all levels. One day I followed Tony LaRussa of the St. Louis Cardinals. His first words to youth coaches: "If we want players to listen to us, we've got to listen to the players." *Right on*, I said to myself.

My first words to youth coaches: "If we pay attention to the players, then we can get the players to pay attention to *themselves.*" You might think that's a tall order, but players have to become aware of what they're doing *before* they can fix it. That's the crucial, and all-too-often ignored, first step of successful coaching.

As adults, we need to pass on our knowledge to the next generation *in a way they can receive it.* And they receive best when they think it's their idea. The coach's task is to point the player's attention to what he is doing so he can consciously reinforce it or find a way to do it differently. That *is* a tall order, but it can happen quite naturally.

In this book, McCarthy says that kids are natural hitters. I agree—my three-year-old son likes to hit things with sticks. As coaches, our job is to help ballplayers unleash their natural swings, and in the process fix their unnatural flaws. Remember, kids are natural *learners*—they learned to walk—without our technical expertise.

John McCarthy suggests that coaches need to do more than just provide a fun and supportive environment; we need to teach this difficult game in an assertive, yet not domineering, manner. That can be a delicate balance, and he is right on the beam here. In that spirit, I offer the Be Your Own Coach recipe for natural coaching: It has served me well over the years as a youth, high-school, and college coach, and I hope it can help you as well. I call it T-I-P:

T for Take Note

Find a way to get the *player* to take note of what he is doing, wrong or right, i.e. stepping forward too far on the swing, stepping away from the target on the throw, whatever. For starters, resist the urge to tell him what he is doing wrong. Catch yourself before you say, "You're doing such and such wrong." Instead *ask* him, "What are you doing with your front foot?" His likely first response may be, "Huh?" Hang in there. Give him a hint. Ask, "Are you stepping here, here, or here?" His likely follow up may be "Duh!" Be patient. If necessary, show him what he *is* doing, *not* what he needs to do to fix it. Let *him* learn what he is doing. The key is that *he* notices the mistake. As soon as he gets what he is doing "wrong," he will try something different. Often he will fix it himself (and you will look like a genius).

I for Improve

In this book, McCarthy emphasizes improvement. As he and I agree, if a player does not fix a fundamental problem on his own, it is the coach's responsibility to help. Show him some different ways of doing it. Get him to *feel* the difference between this swing and that swing. Most of the time, he will recognize the new and different, better swing. He will love it (and you) and will be excited to practice his learning. If he does not and insists that his old, ineffective way is the right way, give him a reality check (i.e. "Are you hitting the ball well this way?"). Get him on board and go forward. It's about him learning how to learn. As he learns, he will perform better.

P for Practice

Finally, have him review the learning in your presence: "Show me the difference between overstriding and your new stride." Now, as John might say, encourage him to practice in your absence. If he does, he is well on his way to being his own version of a player-coach. Because he learned the skill "on his own," he will be able to repeat it when the game is on the line. It will stick with him. Then, as coaches, we can rest assured that we did our best by demanding the player's attention and helping him put that learning into action.

That's the kind of satisfaction John speaks of so eloquently in this gem of a book. It's the kids' "job" to have fun. It's our job, as coaches, to help them learn, learn *how* to learn, and perform under pressure. That is what coaching youngsters is all about. It's their game. Coach them to *be your own coach!* With this book, you'll be well on your way.

02

PREFACE

"What's he doing wrong?" The expression on Dave's face was dead serious, very concerned. I could hear the frustration in his voice. His son was ten years old. As a nine year old the season before, he had not gotten a hit, not one. Now, a few weeks into the new season, he was still not hitting. Dave pleaded, "It's really beginning to bother him. What can I do?"

I can't tell you how many times I've been asked these questions. And why not? Baseball is a popular sport, and most parents want their kids to have fun with it and to do well. And some just don't want to be embarrassed in front of other parents.

The trouble with baseball's popularity is that a lot of coaches are needed, but too few are trained or knowledgeable. When I started thirty years ago, I knew nothing about coaching. Very few parents do when they first volunteer to coach a team. Fortunately, they do volunteer, but often they don't understand the basics or don't know how to teach them.

I went to a bookstore for help, but many books were about big league baseball, written by big league experts. Coaching five- to twelve year-old kids is completely different. Their needs are different. Big league coaches only deal with yesterday's Little League all-stars. They have no idea how to get a below average ten year old to hang in there. I remember wishing that there was a good book for parent-coaches, one that explained the special needs of children, written so that a parent could easily understand.

After all, parents are the ones who most influence whether a boy or girl will improve and stay with the game. That's right: we parents! We're the ones who decide not to drive them to practice, and if the field is too far away, they don't play ... maybe never play. Or, when sign-up time comes and they are a bit hesitant, our lack of support ends the question. On the other hand, if we decide to throw a few pitches to our kids at an early age, one day we may find we have a ballplayer in the family. Most importantly, the parent can help a kid to believe that he is a hitter and that hitting baseballs is easy and fun. By knowing a few basics, you can help mold a good bat swing, or at least prevent bad habits from developing. I've seen some bad habits that take years to fix.

In today's youth baseball circles, parents have gotten a bad reputation. I chatted with a lifelong friend of my father's about this book. "Uncle Load" was always a good athlete and spent his later years coaching and administering youth sports. He laughed and told me, "Jackie, when it comes to parents, there are two rules. The first rule is 'No parents,' and the second rule is 'Remember the first rule.'" In fact, when the subject comes up in conversation, people say, "Yeah, too bad about the way parents act—it ruins everything."

Then it occurred to me that in all my years of coaching, I rarely had a parent problem. I figured it must be because I involved parents from the start. I got them directly involved with the coaching. I'd tell them what to do and what to look for. They became a knowledgeable part of the team, and best of all, they learned how to coach their children on their own.

I'm not saying that just being supportive is not doing enough. It is more than many kids get from their folks. But you can go further if you want to, much further. This book gives you that option. It will help you to be a pretty decent coach if you want to be one, but it also gives you enough background just to help your child improve and hang in there. Whatever you do, it's going to make a difference. You will feel like a better parent, and your son will become a better ballplayer. Best of all, you and your child will become friends, just from playing together.

I coached my older son in Little League for six years. Then, after a six-year stint as coach of my daughter's soccer team, I returned to baseball to coach my younger son. I've also coached basketball and football. My latest experience is with wrestling (coaching my grandson).

Over the years I've learned a great deal about kids and parents. I've also learned lots of hints, tips, and gimmicks on how to get kids going and get them to improve. These tips are all here in this book. They work! All of the teams I have coached have been winning teams, including several championship teams. My baseball teams were always known for their hitting. Not that I emphasize winning. I don't. I emphasize confidence, improvement, and team spirit. These things lead to winning.

I'm convinced there is a good way to get every single kid hitting if he wants to and to help him feel good about his ability. That's why I coach, that's why I wrote this book.

—Jack McCarthy

PLAY BALL!

To a wide-eyed three-year-old, baseball is only about fun, not rules. It all begins with Dad or Mom lobbing a ball. After what seems like a million swings and misses with, mercifully, an oversized plastic bat, suddenly contact is made, and the universe erupts in shouts, bells, and whistles. The child instinctively knows to run, somewhere, anywhere, and then get back to home base before getting caught. That's baseball to the three-year-old, and if you think about it, that's the essence of baseball to all of us. It's a simple game: hit and run.

1–1. AMERICA'S GREATEST PASTIME

After a while, that youngster starts to hang around the field where some big shot seven year olds play, with their fancy Little League or Tee-ball hats. He may get a chance to run down some foul balls. One day the older kids find themselves a player short and ask the rookie to play right field. And magically, a baseball player is born. The sandlot game has remained simple. No umps, no walks, put the ball over the plate, ties go to the runner, use imaginary runners, if needed. Soon, the now five year old stands in full uniform, wobbly-kneed in the batter's box, butterflies in his stomach, feeling he is about to do the most important thing in his life … and both loving and dreading the moment. It's a rite of passage.

It was a simple game in the early days of organized baseball, from the Civil War era up to the forming of the professional leagues at the turn of the twentieth century. Competition has forced the development of more rules to lessen heated disputes. But the love affair between kids of all ages and baseball has much to do with its simplicity, and it's still very much the game of that wide-eyed three year old.

ORIGINS OF BASEBALL

I'm sure that long ago a caveman grabbed his club and smacked a stone across a field or over a tree, and at that moment baseball was born. Hitting round things with sticks was surely a primordial sport. Most agree that modern baseball evolved from an offshoot of English cricket called *rounders*. In rounders, batters hit an underhand pitch and run around four bases or posts placed similar to a baseball diamond, except that home base is a bit farther away from the batter's box. A batter must swing at any pitch he can hit; there are no balls or strikes. The baseball version of the game became popular in America in the mid-eighteenth century. The name *base-ball* was first found in a children's book in 1744. The game was also called *townball*. Basically, a batter had to hit a pitched ball and then run from one to five bases without being tagged or *plugged*—hit by the ball thrown by one of the fielders. Ouch!

Although many credit Abner Doubleday with inventing the modern game, most now agree that it was actually Alexander Joy Cartwright, in 1845, with his set of rules and his design for the modern field layout and dimensions. Cartwright's rules of play were similar to those of the modern game. However, pitching was still underhanded, plugging was still allowed, and a ball caught after only one hop was an out. The first team to score twenty-one *aces* (runs) won, no matter how many innings it took.

The first recorded baseball game was played in 1846 at the Elysian Fields in Hoboken, New Jersey, between Cartwright's amateur New York Knickerbockers and the New York

Baseball Club. These amateur games became more frequent and quite popular. It was a gentleman's game. The batter would signal where he wanted the ball and the pitcher would comply. In 1857, twenty-five teams met to discuss rules; in 1858, they formed the National Association of Base Ball Players, the first organized baseball league. Originally a *ball* was awarded only if the ball was pitched over the batter's head, or if it bounced before crossing home plate. A *walk* was not awarded until nine balls were called. The gentleman's game of underhand pitching and mitten gloves began to evolve. The strike zone was introduced in 1860 to speed games up. Financial pressures arose, and in 1869 the Cincinnati Red Stockings became the first professional team. The rival National (1876) and American (1903) Leagues soon followed and competed in the first World Series in 1903.

Around the turn of the century, in the so-called *dead-ball era*, baseball was a game of single hits, defense, and sharp baserunning. Balls were poorly constructed, and they were used as long as they held together, rain or mud notwithstanding. When the livelier ball was introduced in the 1920s, the modern power game of Babe Ruth emerged. But the old-style game was a great one, and was most poignantly captured in Ty Cobb's autobiography *My Life in Baseball: The True Record*. He wrote:

> Split a finger in those days and you stuck it in the dirt and kept going. In 1907, old Bennet Park in Detroit, as well as other arenas, sprouted grass which was like a cow pasture, rough and rutted with holes and soft spots. Where the infield grass met the skinned infield area, there were drop-offs that sent the ball flying in all directions. Diamonds were given a once over maybe once a week with a rake. Drainage was crude and on wet days the outfield was marshy, if not worse. In the old-time clubhouses we had nothing. Whirlpool baths, electrotherapy, skilled trainers and such were luxuries the Wagners, LaJoies, Speakers, and Mathewsons never experienced. We put our uniforms on in primitive quarters, waited in line for the single shower to be vacated, and dressed the next day in damp uniforms. That's right—damp, if not wet. Uniforms were jammed into containers after a game in their natural sweat-soaked state and seldom saw a laundry. We wore them until they were a grimy disgrace. We had no batting cages, motion pictures to record our form, pitching machines, coaching specialists, and multi-vitamin tablets. The pancake gloves we wore, the washboard fields we played on, the cramped upper berths we climbed into on endless rides over poor railbeds, the need to wrestle with your own luggage, the four-men-to-one bathtub system in hotels, and the crude equipment. ... For instance, bases were left out there until they were spiked apart. They weren't anchored or strapped down firmly and would shift a foot or more when you slid.

01

Pitchers doused the ball with licorice, talcum, slippery elm, and saliva flavored with tobacco. ... If you tore a muscle or broke a bone, a long layoff was out of the question. You played whether you were sick, lame, or half blind from pain. The men I jousted with in the early years were a strange breed never to be seen again. To them, baseball was a way of life, their reason for existence.

THE NEGRO LEAGUES

Our great American pastime was not always so noble. Until 1947, when Jackie Robinson broke the color barrier and played for the Brooklyn Dodgers, baseball mirrored the racial segregation of its surrounding society. Segregation of players based upon race began when the National Association of Base Ball Players on December 11, 1868, voted unanimously to bar "any club which may be composed of one or more colored persons." The first black professional team was the Cuban Giants in 1885; the Negro National League was formed by Rube Foster in 1920. Over four thousand men played in this and subsequent Negro Leagues until 1948.

THE MODERN GAME

The modern game began around 1950. After World War II, black Americans were allowed to play, and baseball also ventured into a new area—night baseball. Lights at parks allowed the games to become accessible to those working during the day. Baseball also started to make its way into homes by radio and later by television. Countless fans, young and old, could now listen to the exploits of their baseball heroes. The 1960s and 1970s ushered in an era of expansion, and many new teams joined the American and National Leagues. New stadiums were built with more seats and less field space (to allow more runs to score). The last thirty years have seen continued expansion. Labor disputes caused baseball to suffer through strikes. Steroids have also darkened perceptions. The fans have responded by staying away for periods of time, but certain players have stepped up to restore interest in the game. Cal Ripken Jr. did it by breaking Lou Gehrig's record for consecutive games played. Mark McGwire and Sammy Sosa did it by breaking Roger Maris's single-season home run record.

Okay, enough history! Let's talk youth baseball. For detailed information about the basics you must know, write to Little League International Baseball and Softball, 539 U.S. Route 15 Hwy, P.O. Box 3485, Williamsport, Pennsylvania, 17701. Ask for a copy of the official Little League rules. You can also look them up at www.littleleague.org. There are many excellent youth baseball organizations, such as the Babe Ruth League, and Cal Ripken Baseball. I refer to Little League since I coached it for nearly twenty years and find their rules very good. If your local club is affiliated with another organization, ask the president for a set of rules. I've also included a glossary of terms at the end of the book so you can start speaking the language of baseball.

A CAPSULE DESCRIPTION OF THE GAME

Baseball is a game where players use a bat to hit pitched balls onto a field of play. When a batter gets a hit, he then tries to run around a diamond-shaped infield touching each of four bases without being tagged out. Upon touching home base, the player scores a run. The team with the most runs at the end is the winner.

The defense tries to get players out before they score. They do so by retrieving the batted ball and then tagging the runner with it or by tagging a base toward which a runner is forced to advance. Upon touching a base, a player is safe. However, he is forced to advance to the next base if runners behind him must advance to his base. (I'll deal with the concept of forced outs in more detail later).

An out occurs when the batter gets three strikes; that is, the batter fails to hit the ball safely with three swings. A strike is also charged by the umpire when a batter fails to swing at a good pitch, or if the ball is hit into foul territory (except when there are already two strikes; then, the count remains unchanged). Additionally, a batter is out if a hit ball is caught by a defender before it touches the ground. Finally, outs are made, as noted above, when a runner is tagged between bases or when a player with the ball touches a base to which the runner must advance.

Teams alternate on offense and defense. The game is divided into nine innings. When each team has had a chance to bat, one inning is completed. Once a team has made three outs in its half of the inning, the next team gets up at bat. If the score is tied after nine innings, the game continues until an inning ends with one team ahead.

A player must advance to first base after hitting a fair ball that touches the ground before being caught. The batter also will advance to first base with a walk—if the pitcher throws the ball outside the strike zone four times. Normally, the player may advance to second, third, and home base at his own risk and may steal the next base if he can avoid being tagged. If a prior base is empty, a player does not need to advance upon a hit ball. When the player is safe on a base, the next batter gets up to hit. Nine players on each team are allowed on the field and in the batting order at one time. However, most youth leagues provide that all kids present are in the batting lineup.

FIELD DIMENSIONS AND GENERAL RULES

A Little League field is small compared to big league fields. Players up to twelve years old play on a field about two-thirds the size of a big league field. (See figure 1-2.) Little League bases are 60 feet apart, about the same distance as on an adult softball field. In the professional major leagues, the bases are a long 90 feet apart. Kids move to the 90-foot length at thirteen to fourteen years of age. This is usually a difficult adjustment. To ease the transition, some clubs use a 75-foot basepath for thirteen year olds.

The pitcher pitches from a rubber mat, the front of which is 46 feet from the back point of home plate, as opposed to 60 feet 6 inches in the big leagues. In the early days of baseball, the pros pitched from 46 feet. It was a gentleman's game then, and pitches were firm but underhand. When competition increased the speed of pitching in the

1-2. REGULATION LITTLE LEAGUE FIELD

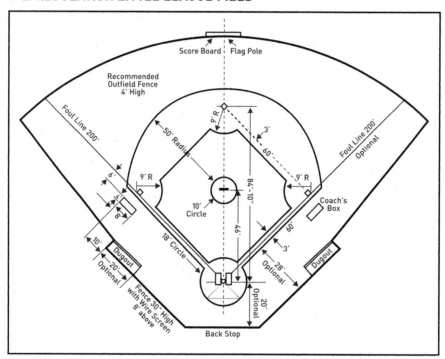

Official Little League field layout. All dimensions are compulsory unless marked "Optional." In some leagues for twelve year olds, the bases are 70 feet apart, and the distance from the front of the pitcher's rubber to the back of home plate is 50 feet. For tournament play, outfield fences may be expanded to 210 to 220 feet.

6

1880s, the mound was pushed back to its current spot. Little League fences are usually about 180 to 200 feet from home plate, while professional league fences average about 350 to 400 feet. Often, neighborhood fields for the youngest kids have no fences, so on a hot summer day, a hard grounder can roll a mile on the baked ground.

In 2007, the Babe Ruth League field expanded for twelve year olds to *50-70*, that is, 50 feet for pitching (pitcher's rubber to the plate) and 70 feet to each base. Overall, this change seems to add more excitement to the game and eases the transition to big league field dimensions. However, I'm quite concerned about the tendency to do this at the ten- and eleven-year-old levels, which is far too young. Kids' arms wear out faster with the longer pitch, and stealing becomes a too dominant part of play. Little League has not made this change yet, but I noted that the outfield fences were moved back 20 feet to about 215 to 220 feet at the official field in Williamsport, Pennsylvania. It is hoped that this will increase the number of doubles and triples in youth baseball tournament play—a welcome move! Of course, it may take a while for local clubs to adjust their fences to accommodate such changes. Some clubs in my area play the 50-70 diamond on the Major League-sized fields used by older kids. They simply move home plate 10 feet closer to the mound; however, this still leaves unreachable 300-feet fences to contend with.

The distance from home plate to the backstop is optional. Young players need a close backstop since younger catchers errantly let many pitches go by (called *passed balls*). Thus, there are a lot of stolen bases; local organizations often make rules to try to reduce the stealing, which can tend to dominate the game. As a side note, the backstop at Yankee Stadium is 82 feet behind home plate; however, at Boston's Fenway Park it's only 60 feet, which is one of several reasons why Fenway is such a great hitter's park. When there is less foul territory, fewer foul pop-ups are caught.

YOUR LOCAL CLUB

Youth baseball is enjoyed by youngsters from five to eighteen years of age. Local town clubs may be affiliated with a large national association, such as Little League or the Babe Ruth League, or may just adopt their own rules without any national affiliation. Tee-ball, as discussed further in chapter six, generally includes five to six year olds in Little League, and four to six year olds in the Cal Ripken Division of Babe Ruth Baseball. Thereafter, most leagues will have a minor league and a major league division for kids from seven to twelve years of age, with the minors including seven to ten year olds and the majors usually ranging from ten to twelve year olds. There are additional variations

01

in both minor and major league divisions from league to league; for instance, some clubs will just field teams within each individual age for ten to twelve year olds. Junior and Senior divisions are often available for thirteen to fifteen and sixteen to eighteen year olds, respectively. The variations are substantial, so parents need to inquire with their local club regarding the organization and opportunities available for children of different ages.

How children get placed on teams also varies from town to town. Call a club official if you need to know this information. For beginners, the teams are put together by club officials. They may call kids to a "tryout" where each child is rated on a point scale. Then, they give each team the same number of above- and below-average players. The coaches may already be familiar with the kids from Tee-ball, and may tryout only new players. The officials do their best, but you never know until the umpire says, "Play ball!" how well a kid can or will do.

At the nine- or ten-year-old level, the coaches usually get together and draft their teams just like in the pros. They have the kids' ratings from last year and their own notes. More experienced coaches, or ones like me who coach several sports, usually know the best talent. We draw lots to see who chooses first and then select in rotation. After teams are picked, there may be some trading to accommodate various local issues.

Little League games last for six innings, light permitting. Little League rules require every player on the roster to play at least six defensive outs (two innings) and bat at least one time. Some clubs require the coach to bat every player in the game in rotation. At the Tee-ball level, all the kids bat in order and play at least half the game on defense. Check with your local board and get a copy of the rules concerning your club. Some clubs follow official Little League rules; others are independent and make up their own. If a coach violates these rules, particularly as to playing time, a parent should talk to him or call the club president.

BEGINNER-, INTERMEDIATE-, AND ADVANCED-LEVEL PLAY

We will often refer in this book to the various levels of play, usually beginner, intermediate, and advanced. There are no hard and fast rules on the ages that distinguish a kid's level of play; it depends both on ability and prior years of play. Generally, beginner ball is the level for all kids below nine years of age. After that we expect at least intermediate-level play until age eleven, and advanced play after that. Any kid in his first year, no matter what his age, will be at a beginner level for a while.

8

Kids start playing Tee-ball by five or six years old. I've seen four year olds play. They face some live pitching from coaches by age seven or eight. (I saw a team try to have kids pitch to each other at six, and it was a disaster.) By eight or nine, the better players will be asked to play on All-Star or traveling teams to play other towns. Teams of eleven to twelve year olds, often called the *Major Leagues* in youth ball, are the pinnacle of Little League play. These teams play the popular Little League World Series against other nations in Williamsport, Pennsylvania. For thirteen-year-olds, the field dimensions expand, and by fourteen, in high school, the kids are playing on regular Major League-sized fields. Of course, All-Star teams are quickly exposed to advanced-level play.

PERSONAL TRAINERS

The last few years have seen a great increase in the use of personal trainers in many, if not most, sports. At one time, personal trainers were the exclusive province of sports such as figure skating and gymnastics. Now, more and more in baseball, we see trainers hired by small groups and even individually. My reaction initially was that it was a bit much. In high school, scholarship opportunities make it more important for players to get an edge, but prior to that I feel the primary goal should be to have fun. Somehow, the notion of a personal trainer seems to bring a level of competitiveness beyond what should be in the game at that level. However, the cat has been let out of the bag, and the practice is becoming extensive. If a kid is a good athlete, a personal trainer will make him better; for a great athlete, it can make the difference in bringing his game to college- or pro-level play.

That being said, lack of a personal trainer does not doom a kid to not getting a scholarship, and hard work, encouragement, and practice nonetheless will ensure improvement.

BATTING RULES

A batter must stand in the *batter's box*. This is a rectangle 3 feet 8 inches wide by 8 feet 8 inches long, starting 27½ inches behind the back tip of the plate and set 4 inches away (6 inches in the pros) from the side of the plate. There is one on each side of the plate, one for righties and one for lefties. A batter must be entirely inside the box while hitting the ball. Often, youth baseball fields are not *lined*, and there is only an imaginary batter's box. I like to tell kids to stand as far back in the batter's box as the umpire will allow. Using the entire length of 27½ inches gives the batter a split second longer to see the ball, and it seems to shrink the strike zone. As noted, the batter's box ends 4 inches away from the side of the plate. A batter who crosses that line, especially by stepping on or in front of the plate when he swings, is out upon hitting the ball. (See figure 1-3.)

The *strike zone* is the area over home plate from the batter's knees to his armpits when he assumes a natural batting stance. If any part of a pitched ball passes through this area, the batter will be charged with a *strike*. (See figure 1-4 on page 11.)

Three strikes are an out. Strike zones often vary by umpires, and this is the source of many arguments in baseball. Over the years, the strike zone has varied widely in the pros, with the upper part of the zone moving up and down from the neck to the

1–3. REGULATION BATTER'S BOX

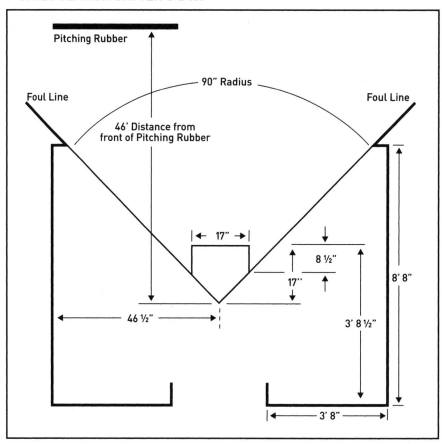

Official Little League layout of batter's box and compulsory dimensions.

1-4. THE STRIKE ZONE

strike
zone

Little League Rule 2.00: The strike zone is that space over home plate that is between the batter's armpits and the top of the knees when the batter assumes a natural batting stance. The umpire shall determine the strike zone according to the batter's usual stance when that batter swings at a pitch. When any part of the ball passes through any part of the strike zone, a strike is called.

waist. A pitch outside the strike zone is called a *ball*. Four balls in one at bat is called a *walk*, which entitles the batter to go to first base.

It kills me when coaches or parents yell, "A walk is as good as a hit," or "Swing only if it's good." Sure, with a 3-0 count (three balls, no strikes) I agree. With three balls, the batter has a good chance to earn a free base on a walk and should try to do so. Other than that, parents and coaches should always encourage a child to hit the ball. Don't encourage a kid to seek a walk just because he is a typically poor hitter. It may be good for those who think winning is important, but the message to the player is, "Take a walk, kid, because we don't have much faith in your bat." If you don't have faith in him, he'll never find self-confidence. Encourage kids to swing and to seek a good pitch instead.

FAIR AND FOUL BALLS

A runner advances to first base, or beyond, upon a batted ball that lands in fair territory. The *foul territory* is the area outside the two foul lines. The foul lines run along the first and third baselines and extend out to the boundaries of the field, usually a fence. A *foul ball* is a batted ball that lands in foul territory. The first two foul balls count as strikes, but the third does not advance the count, since a batter can't strike out on a foul ball. A foul tip is a ball nicked by the bat, and also counts as a foul ball. However, the batter is out if the catcher catches a foul tip on what would be the third strike.

Here are the basic "fair and foul" rules:

- A batted ball that passes first or third base and lands in fair territory is a fair ball.
- A ball that touches a foul line or a foul pole is still fair.
- A batted ball that touches in fair territory and then rolls foul before it gets to first or third base is a foul ball as soon as the fielder retrieves it.
- A batted ball that touches in fair territory and rolls foul after it passes any part of first or third base, even if it just grazes the outside corner of the base, is a fair ball.
- If a player touches the ball in fair territory and then it goes foul, it is a fair ball.
- If a batted ball rolls into foul territory in the infield area, and then rolls back into fair territory, it is a fair ball.

Misunderstandings of this rule are usually good for a groan or two from parents during a game.

BASERUNNING RULES

A runner is *forced* and must advance to the next base if he is on first base or if the bases behind him are filled and a hit ball touches fair ground. So if a runner is on first, he must go to second; if runners are on first and second, both must advance, and so forth. However, if a runner is on second, and no one is on first, then he is not forced and can stay on second base if it would be dangerous to try to advance (for example, on a ground ball hit toward third base). (See figure 1-5 A, B on page 13.)

If the ball is hit up in the air, the runner should not advance too far until the ball is caught or missed. If the ball is caught in flight, the runner must *tag up*, which means he must retouch (or remain on) the base he was on at the time of the pitch. If a fielder with the ball touches the base or the runner before the runner tags up, the runner is out. This is also called being *doubled up*, and often happens when an infield line drive is caught. After a legal tag up, a runner may attempt to advance, even if the ball was caught in foul territory. This often happens with a runner at third when a fly ball is caught deep in the outfield. The runner can usually go back and touch third base and still get home before the throw gets to the catcher.

1-5. THE FORCE PLAY

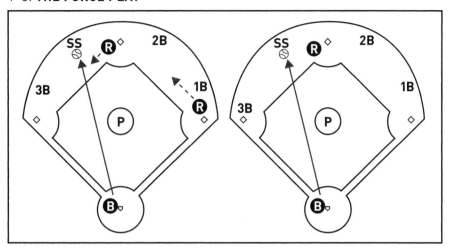

A: The runners on first and second are "forced" on a ground ball and must try to advance to the next base. They are out if any fielder with the ball in hand touches them or that next base before the runner arrives.

B: In this instance, the runner on second is not forced and may stay safely on the base.

Running into or obstructing a fielder who is trying to make a play or moving in a manner to hinder or distract a batter is called *interference*. In the first instance, the runner is out and the other runners return to the last base they touched. The ball is dead. In the latter case, the umpire warns the player to stop. If a fielder interferes with a runner, it is called *obstruction*.

The *infield fly rule* prevents infielders from intentionally dropping a pop-up to get a double play. The rule is that if the ball can be caught by an infielder with ordinary effort, when there are runners on first and second or bases are loaded with none or one out, the batter is automatically out and runners can tag up and advance at their own risk. (See figure 1-6 on page 14.) If the ball is dropped, the runners do not need to advance (since the batter is out and there is no force play). Many Little League umpires do not use this rule. I think they just forget to call it, or they don't understand it.

Players are allowed to *steal* a base under certain conditions. A steal occurs when a player advances other than upon a batted ball, i.e., usually after a *passed ball*, or in other words, a pitch missed by the catcher. Because the distance between bases is so short, Little League runners are not allowed to take a *lead* (step off the base). They can only leave the base when the pitched ball reaches the batter. A runner who leaves

1-6. THE INFIELD FLY RULE

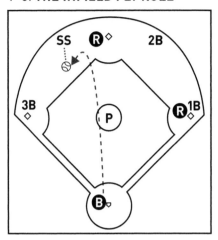

A complicated rule. If runners are on first and second, or bases are loaded, with no outs or one out, and a catchable infield pop-up is hit that could be caught with ordinary effort, then the runners are not forced if the fielder drops the ball. The batter is automatically out. The idea is to prevent fielders from intentionally dropping the ball, perhaps for an easy double play.

the base before the pitch reaches the batter must go back. He is not automatically out. If the ball is hit, the runner must go back to the base, or to the next unoccupied base. Local rules sometimes prohibit stealing completely or prohibit stealing home.

As noted above, some leagues have adopted different rules for twelve year olds that increase field dimensions and provide for longer basepaths. (All-Star teams of ten- or eleven year olds are also beginning to use these larger fields, at least occasionally.) Runners in these leagues are able to steal at any time.

The runner is out if a batted ball hits the runner, if the runner interferes with a fielder, or if the runner doesn't slide into a base when the fielder at the base has the ball.

TIE GAMES

Tie regulation games that are halted by the umpire due to weather, curfew, or lack of light are resumed at the same point where they were stopped, if four innings have been completed. If one team is ahead at that time, or if the home team is ahead or tied after three and a half innings, it is a regulation game. If a game has not reached four innings, or has reached three and a half innings with the home team losing, it is declared no game, and all scores are erased. The game is played over.

HITTING

Hitting is the essence of baseball, and is clearly the most fun. An old ballplayer once told me, "Defense is what you do while you're waiting to get at bat again." Sure, fielding, running, and throwing are big parts of the game, no doubt about it, but hitting is why people play.

Anyone who has ever hit a home run, or seen a loved one do so, knows what I mean. For a moment, time stops. Everyone is breathless, watching the ball against the sky as it fights wind currents, and then, as it floats down, all eyes strain to see if it will clear the fence. As it drops from sight, the quiet awe is suddenly shattered by a triumphant roar rising from the crowd.

So, when it comes to baseball skills, hitting is where we start. Many coaches, especially big league coaches, will say that either you have it as a hitter or you don't.

2-1. HITTING: THE ESSENCE OF BASEBALL

See the ball in the top, right corner.

15

They will quote statistics showing that a player's average is generally highest early in his pro career, suggesting there is usually little or no improvement from year to year. Well, that may be true for the big leagues, maybe even for college, and perhaps high school (though I doubt it). But it is absolutely dead wrong for children. Kids can improve tremendously. I've seen it countless times. I've also seen kids who are bad hitters get much worse. This tells me loud and clear: Coaching helps, and parents count. Encouragement and practice can make the difference.

CONFIDENCE: YA GOTTA BELIEVE!

This is the most important concept in this whole book. If hitting is the heart of baseball, then confidence is its soul. If you can help your players *believe* they are good hitters, so that they *expect* to hit the ball when they get up to bat, then you have planted a seed whose growth cannot be denied. A kid at bat should be thinking about *where* the ball will go, not *whether* he will hit it. There is a technique to raising a kid's hitting confidence, and it's easier than you may think.

You have to tell kids they are already hitters.

There is a hitter inside each of them, maybe still waiting to come out, maybe needing some help, some instruction, some experience, but definitely a hitter. At my first practice each year, that's just what I do. I tell my players they *are* hitters. I have them say it. I keep saying it. Sports psychologists tell us positive affirmation works. I have thirty years of coaching experience, and I have seen it work countless times. As a coach, you should pitch to a struggling hitter from up close until he starts making contact, then gradually move farther away. I make a fuss when someone makes good contact with the ball. The sound or *crack* of a well-hit ball is distinctive. I point it out to kids, and pretty soon everybody is listening for it, and everyone is trying to make that sound.

It's no lie, not even a fib, not at the Little League level: *All kids are hitters.* Hitting is easy at the young ages where the ball comes in more slowly; it's very hit-able.

A kid's hitting problem starts with poor batting form and quickly grows as fear or self-doubt takes hold. Never, never, never criticize a player (or your child if you are a parent) in a way that tells him he is not a hitter. If you do, he may never become the hitter he already is. Just say, "You are a hitter, I know you are. We're almost there. It's coming. Ya gotta believe!" Then when it does come (and it will), when he swings the bat nicely or makes good contact (the first sign of improvement), you let the whole world know about it. Make that kid feel proud and confident, and his ability will blossom.

One season, I had a ten-year-old boy on the team who I had coached as an eight year old. I drafted him again because I liked him. This boy was motivated. He wanted to be a good hitter in the worst way. He'd had a tough season the year before, and he was having similar troubles early in this season—swinging too hard, trying too hard. He would strike out and start crying.

I told him it was okay to cry, no problem. It just showed how much he wanted to hit, and that was fine. I kept telling him that he was a hitter, that it was just stuck inside somewhere. I'd say, "Just relax a bit. Control your energy. Swing with confidence. It'll come." And by midseason, it did. The hits came, and, with them, a smile you could float on and a gleam in his mother's eye that sparkled like sunshine. He really *expected* to hit the ball, and when that happens, the hits follow.

02

The worst problem with kids who are not hitting is usually not their style of swinging; that's easy to fix. The main problem is that they do not "see" the ball, often because of some distraction, like fear or doubt. These feelings feed off each other. First, kids may be afraid that the pitcher will hit them. This occurs at about age eight or nine, when kids start doing the pitching. The fear causes a defensive swing, or it makes them step back until they can't even reach the ball. After many hitless at bats, self-doubt takes over. They think they can't do it. They become afraid of being embarrassed in front of friends and parents. Now they have three problems: fear, self-doubt, *and* a lousy swing. They are certainly not focused on the ball. You have to face these problems head on. Tell a fearful batter he can do it, that it's easy, that he's a hitter, and that improvement is going to come as sure as the morning sun. Ya gotta believe!

Start with just a spark of confidence, then mold a good swing from it. As noted above, pitch from closer in or pitch underhand to get your kid's confidence going. If your players are to believe in themselves, you have to believe in them. Get rid of negatives, focus on the positive, and things will happen the way they are supposed to happen. Good hitters think it's easy to hit; ask them—they are the ones who know!

HITTING, HITTING, HITTING

PRACTICE, PRACTICE, PRACTICE

If confidence is the soul of baseball, then repetition is its backbone. I've had many winning teams in baseball and the main reason is *lots* of batting practice. Emphasize hitting! I remember telling one parent after his nine year old was swinging his bat nicely, "He has a nice swing. Now he just needs to hit a few thousand balls." Too often parents just go out and play catch with their child. That's great, but remember that hitting should also be emphasized.

17

The more that a child practices hitting, the better he is going to be, especially at Little League age. Somebody has to pitch to him and practice with him. This is where parents come in. Tell the parents on your team to get a couple of balls and throw to their kids. Using several balls will save time chasing after them, unless you have an eager second child for that task. I use a whole bucket of balls.

Tell Mom or Dad to pitch to the child at home. Tell them not to worry about how well they can pitch—they will improve, too! Throw the ball from a close distance at first, initially from 25 to 35 feet away if that helps control. If the child does not make contact at that distance, move in until the right distance is found. Move back gradually to 46 feet. For kids younger than nine, 35 feet or less is fine. From nine years old and onward, you want to get to 46 feet as soon as possible. (Remember, in Little League games, the pitcher is 46 feet away from the batter.)

Make it fun! With my son Joey, I put a marker on the field for the farthest distance he hit a ball that day. Have your kid try to hit to different fields—right, center, and left. Twenty to thirty pitches at one time is okay: More is better. Mickey Mantle's father used to pitch to him every day, while his brother chased down the balls. Repetition works, guaranteed! It works not only to refine the mechanics, but it also helps with body chemistry, as chapter eight on coaching and winning discusses in detail.

Another great idea is to take your child to a batting cage. Your town or club may have one available at practices. If not, look for a indoors batting center in a nearby city. They are great for rainy days. They usually have slow- and medium-speed cages for children. Forty to forty-five miles per hour is fine for nine to ten year olds. Often, the manager can adjust the speed to accommodate different ages. Eleven and twelve year olds should hit a 50 to 55 miles per hour pitch. Start slow and build up speed. It costs about two bucks for twenty balls. Sixty balls makes a thorough workout and is about the most you should do. Also, kids should use their own bats if they have them—the grips are often lousy on batting cage bats. A batter's glove is also *very* useful, since the hand can get sore from a good workout. Batting cages have helmets—ask for one. Take pictures, and take a break after every twenty balls to talk about the swing or watch other batters. The idea is to do a lot of hitting—that's the key to it all. Have him take some swings lefty (if he is a righty) and bunt a few, too. Give a holler when he makes good contact. Just for fun, take some swings yourself.

THE FUNDAMENTALS OF HITTING

I recall a time in a game twenty years ago when an eight year old got up to the plate. You could see that he was uncomfortable and didn't really know what to do. He chopped at the first pitch for a strike, and his coach started yelling, "C'mon, hit the ball, hit the ball." The next pitch came in, and the boy missed it by more than a foot. Again the coach started screaming, "Hit the ball, c'mon, hit the ball." Finally, the kid turned in frustration and shrieked to his coach, "All right, but how? I'm trying, but how?"

I walked up to the boy. At that age level, the coaches helped each other, and I knew his parents. "No problem. Just keep your eye on it. Watch it leave the pitcher's hand, and watch it until it's in front of you, right over the plate. Don't take your eyes off it." On the next pitch, he hit the ball. He popped out, but he hit the ball. After he turned to go to the dugout, he flashed a big grin at me—it made my day!

Saying general things like "Hit the ball" is not helpful. Yell out some of the basics like "See the whole ball," "Keep your head down," "Swing with confidence," "Keep your hands up," "Hard bat," or "Don't drop your right side." These things are helpful. The next sections discuss such specifics in detail.

It's a big help to be supportive, to raise confidence, and to practice with the kids. If that's all you do, it's still a great help. But the detailed knowledge of the basics of hitting—working with young players on the mechanics of the stance and swing—will reap immediate and permanent rewards. There is clearly a science to hitting, and those who can teach it will see great improvement quickly in their players.

It's very important to observe the batter make a dozen or so swings and to look at the stance, the hands, the eyes, the feet, the bat path, and slowly start to mold good batting form. Too few coaches really take the time to focus on each part of the swing to detect a problem. So, let's get on to it.

KEEP YOUR EYE ON THE BALL

This is without a doubt the most important part of hitting! Most kids don't usually "see" the pitch until it's about one-third of the way to them. They start their swing, maybe turn their heads, and don't really see the ball for the last 5 to 10 feet. They only see the ball for about half of the time it's in flight, less than a split second. There's no way a child is going to hit the ball—not hit it hard anyway—if he doesn't see it well. The most important thing you can say during practice, or at a game when a batter is up, is simply, "Keep your eye on the ball! Watch it leave the pitcher's hand. Watch it all the way to the bat!" (Note the section in chapter nine on how to exercise for better vision.)

There are a couple of hints you should consider using. I remember when my eldest son, Jackie, was nine years old. A boy named Ray was on our team, a big kid, very quiet and not particularly sure of himself. But he had a big heart and wanted to play ball. He hadn't gotten many hits during the first few games. He was tight when he swung, and he didn't swing often. During one game, he had already struck out a few times. He was up late in the game, and the score was close, so I had to get him to swing. I called "time out" from my place coaching third base and went over to talk to him. "Ray, you're a hitter, so I want you to do something for me. I want you to swing at every pitch. This pitcher is good, and he'll get the ball over the plate. Also, I want you to see which way the ball is spinning as it comes toward you, and tell me after each pitch."

Well, he missed the first pitch in the dirt, but took the second pitch over the center fielder's head. He watched the ball in surprise for a full three or four seconds; everybody screamed at him to run. As he finally ran to first base, he turned to me and raised his hand. Pointing his finger, he rotated it in a clockwise direction. He was telling me which way the ball was spinning! We had found a way to get him to look closely at the ball, and he got a big hit. Of course, he took such a long time getting around the bases that he got tagged out at home, but I don't think he ever knew it—everybody was cheering so loudly.

His family moved after the season, and we got Christmas cards for a few years. My wife went back to county college for some courses ten years later and guess who she had in her class—Ray ... as big as a house! He fondly remembered that great home run he hit!

Teaching fundamentals can go a long way. Look at the player's eyes and head when he swings. If he lifts his head or turns his head with his shoulders as he swings, he is not looking at the ball long enough. Tell him to try to see the ball while it's still in the pitcher's hand, to be sure that he watches it from the start. He must also try to see the ball in front of him, over the plate, until the bat hits it. Tell him to keep his head still and try to see the bat hit the ball. He should be looking right down his arms, along the bat. He won't be able to actually see the bat hit the ball, but he'll watch the ball long enough to hit it. Ted Williams used to say he could see the bat hit the ball (I certainly never could!).

So those are the three keys: Watch the ball leave the pitcher's hand, watch it closely enough to see it spin as it comes toward the plate, and try to see it hit the bat. Then tell your player to run, because he will have hit it!

LOOK LIKE A BATTER

The *initial stance* is that batting position assumed when waiting for the pitch. I call it the initial stance because just before the batter swings, he cocks into a *loaded stance*, which is quite a different posture.

The idea behind the stance is to help the batter to see the ball better, and to position his body to quickly and powerfully load up and then deliver the bat into the strike zone. A good stance will keep the swing balanced. While there is a preferred or best stance, there are also many different ways to do it.

If you watch a professional baseball game, you will see about eighteen different stances. All the great players had varied stances. Pete Rose bent over very far so that his head was right in the strike zone. He "saw" the ball better that way, and that's why he is the all-time leader in hits. Many guys, like old-timer Rod Carew, point their bat back at the umpire. They swing very level, slapping out a lot of singles—for a high batting average but no power. Other guys wrap the bat around their heads. Willie Mays spread his legs wide for power, while Babe Ruth and Stan Musial kept their legs close. Some plant the right foot back a bit, some the left. Yankee All-Star Don Mattingly used to "pigeon toe" his back foot a bit to get more power. For some reason, he stopped doing this in 1988, and he never had a great year slugging again. Mel Ott used to lift his left foot up so high that he looked like he was about to fall down. Yankee old-timer Don Baylor liked to get close to the plate to pull the ball to left field. That's why he had the all-time record for being hit by pitches until Craig Biggio recently broke it.

The key to an initial stance is to let the batter be comfortable—this is one area where you give a young player some freedom to do it his way. I'm not saying that there isn't a "right" stance, and there are clearly some very important "don'ts" that I will touch on. However, hitting is less affected by the initial stance than by other things, such as *seeing* the ball, so here is an area where you can allow more room for some personal style. Kids are built differently, so one style may be more comfortable than another.

At very young ages, children try to face you as you pitch the ball. It looks cute, but you must gently insist that they stand sideways. Also, young children tend to hold the bat right in front of the breastbone. For a proper stance, you need to move the hands farther back, near the right shoulder (for righties), with the hands up and even with the shoulder. Make sure the knees are bent a bit. Once you've gone over the basics, tell the batter, "Now you look like a hitter!" Then, when he begins to lapse into an improper stance, just repeat the phrase, "Look like a hitter!" and watch that kid snap into a correct stance. The main thing in a stance is to keep the hands up and back a bit. At the very least, make sure the batter gets this part right.

Some coaches put way too much emphasis on stance. They can really mess up a kid, so that the kid starts to think too much, or gets too stiff, or seems to forget how to swing at all. I've seen coaches do nothing but work on a kid's stance, and by the time they are done, the kid holds the bat like a stone statue and swings as if his feet were stuck in concrete. It's okay to aim for the "correct" stance, particularly if a kid is struggling; just don't try to do too much at once. Work with one thing at a time, from within the framework of the child's present stance. If the kid is hitting well, leave him alone. Focus on the kid who is struggling.

THE TOP TEN KEYS OF A CORRECT INITIAL STANCE

This is for righties. (Do the opposite for lefties.) See figure 2-2 on page 23.

1. Keep the feet shoulder width apart or even a bit wider. If the feet are close together, you get more power, since you take a bigger stride toward the ball. However, this also means the body is lunging more, so you lose some bat control. If the feet are spread wide, you get the opposite—less lunge and less power, but more control. Adjust to what's comfortable, what works best. The key is to feel balanced. Adjust so the legs feel balanced.

2. Stand back in the batter's box. The left foot should never be closer to the pitcher than the infield edge of the plate. Usually, the farther back the batter stands in the batter's box (toward the catcher), the better. The batter will have more time to see the ball, and it also shrinks the strike zone. Of course, if the pitcher is throwing a lot of low pitches, or the umpire has a low strike zone, the batter should move forward (closer to the pitcher) to meet the ball before it drops. Place the feet close enough to the plate so that the end of the bat covers the outside portion of the plate with a few inches to spare.

3. The right foot can be set even with the left, but preferably, set it an inch or so back. Some players whose dominant eye is the back eye (the right eye for a righty hitter) will open the stance a bit more so they can see better with that eye. See chapter nine for how to identify the dominant eye. The back foot should be pointed straight ahead or even pigeon-toed a bit for more power.

4. The weight should be on the balls of the toes, with a bit more weight on the back foot. Sometimes I stick a glove or a bat under the right heel to keep it up so the weight is more on the toes. Flat-footedness is a no-no; it causes a jerky swing with less power and control. Again, stress balance. The hitter wants to feel springy—balanced but ready to pop.

2-2. **THE STANCE**

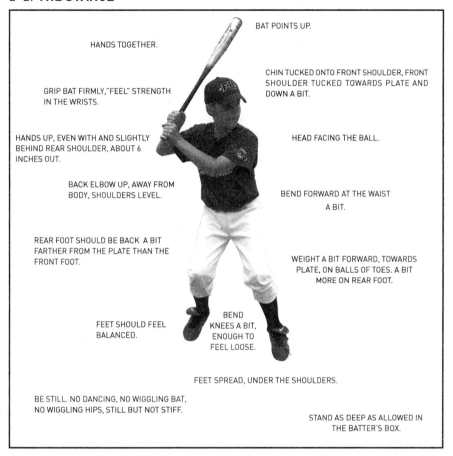

BAT POINTS UP.

HANDS TOGETHER.

CHIN TUCKED ONTO FRONT SHOULDER, FRONT SHOULDER TUCKED TOWARDS PLATE AND DOWN A BIT.

GRIP BAT FIRMLY, "FEEL" STRENGTH IN THE WRISTS.

HEAD FACING THE BALL.

HANDS UP, EVEN WITH AND SLIGHTLY BEHIND REAR SHOULDER, ABOUT 6 INCHES OUT.

BACK ELBOW UP, AWAY FROM BODY, SHOULDERS LEVEL.

BEND FORWARD AT THE WAIST A BIT.

REAR FOOT SHOULD BE BACK A BIT FARTHER FROM THE PLATE THAN THE FRONT FOOT.

WEIGHT A BIT FORWARD, TOWARDS PLATE, ON BALLS OF TOES. A BIT MORE ON REAR FOOT.

FEET SHOULD FEEL BALANCED.

BEND KNEES A BIT, ENOUGH TO FEEL LOOSE.

FEET SPREAD, UNDER THE SHOULDERS.

BE STILL. NO DANCING, NO WIGGLING BAT, NO WIGGLING HIPS, STILL BUT NOT STIFF.

STAND AS DEEP AS ALLOWED IN THE BATTER'S BOX.

It is helpful for the coach to look at each part of a batter's stance to see if there are any flaws. Start at the feet and work upward, point by point.

5. Bend the knees as much as is comfortable. The idea is to be loose, to have the feeling of balance. Some pros bend the knees very low, to shrink the strike zone, but I feel it sacrifices balance. Also bend forward from the waist a little bit. This helps the batter to loosen up, keeps the weight forward on the balls of the toes, and gets the head closer to the strike zone to see the ball.

6. Use a light bat. Make sure the bat is not too heavy. Today's pros have gotten away from the big, heavy bats used in the old days. The bats are still big, but the grips are thinned out. This allows them to whip the bats around very quickly. Bat speed is important, so have your players start off with a lighter bat. See the discussion on page 37 on buying a bat.

Everything has its exception, and so it's possible to have too light a bat. In 1989, I had a big kid who was having trouble making contact. His dad was helping me to coach, and I told him the problem was mainly mechanical. One day at pregame batting practice, I told the kid to get a heavier bat. Then he started making contact! During the game, he smashed a screaming double, went two for three, and won the game. So, sometimes you have to experiment. Tell the kids to try different bats in batting practice. They will figure out pretty quickly what bat works for them, under your close guidance. Also, have them *choke up*—grip the bat a few inches above the knob at the bottom of the bat. They need to be in complete control of the bat. Make sure they *don't* interlock fingers, even if the golfer in the family thinks it's a good idea.

7. The grip holding the bat should be relaxed, not a squeeze, but mildly firm. For righties, the right hand is on top of the left, opposite for lefties. Moving the fingers a bit helps loosen and relax the hands. Tell the batter to "feel" the strength in the wrist and forearm through his fingers into the bat. There are different ways to place the hands in relation to each other. In the most normal grip, the largest finger bones (just past the knuckles) on both hands are all in a line. This grip gives both power and control. For more power, separate the wrists a bit. The knuckles of the top hand are then directly above the largest finger bones of the lower hand. This draws in the forearms and shoulders for more power. (See figure 2-3 on page 25.) For more control, you can use a loose grip. Bring the wrists closer together with the large, mid-finger joints lined up. This looser grip tends to give a lot more control, relying more on the wrist and the fingers. It also gives more snapping wrist action and helps the batter make contact control. The power grip also relies mainly on fingers but brings in the palm pads under the main knuckles. In any case, the bat barely touches the bottom of the palm of the hand. Fingers do the job. The hands should be together, an inch or so from the bottom of the bat.

8. The hands should be kept up. They should be by the right shoulder, never lower than the top of the strike zone, with the arms relaxed. I like to see the hands right in front of the back shoulder, about 4 to 6 inches out. Holding the bat too low is a part of the stance you *must* change—hands have to be up, but not too high; the top of the shoulder is fine. Hands should not be too far back to be uncomfortable. The bat should point up, either back a bit toward the catcher, or even forward a bit. Just make

A: Loose Grip. Mid-finger knuckles lined up, wrists closer. Good for control, slapping singles.

B: Normal Grip. The large finger bones are lined up. This is where you start.

C: Power Grip. Separate wrists a bit more. Main knuckles on top hand are over large finger joints on lower hand. Closed grip gives more power.

sure it's not wrapped back behind the head; there's no need for the top of the bat to travel farther than necessary. Some kids like to wrap it around the head or sit it on the shoulder; they *must* change this. The less distance the head of the bat has to drop to get to the top of the strike zone, the better.

9. The right elbow should be up a little and away from the body, but it shouldn't be so high as to be uncomfortable. This is important. Many kids start the swing with their back elbow and upper arm too close and tight to the body or too high. The whole right side will drop, causing a golf-like uppercut swing, one of the more difficult problems to cure. Stop it early! The swing must be level, and one key to a level swing is hand and elbow position. Keep the back shoulder up. The slightly raised back elbow

2-4. **IMPROPER STANCES**

A: Facing home plate, left leg open too much.

B: Hands are too low and not back by shoulder.

C: Bat sitting on shoulder.

D: Stance too far forward, past plate.

E: Stiff-legged, weight on back of feet.

F: Hands reversed, right hand should be on top.

G: Bat wrapped around the head.

keeps the shoulders level. A level swing has a much better chance of hitting the ball. This is one of the keys, and it must be emphasized. Make sure that the angle between the upper arm and the right side of the chest is 45 degrees or more.

10. The head should fully face the pitcher, chin tucked in near the left shoulder. The left shoulder is tucked in a bit toward the plate. The eyes are focused on the spot where the pitcher will release the ball, at the top of his stretch. It's important to keep the head stationary (just as in golf).

Now the batter is ready. One more thing—the body must be still. Any unnecessary motion can cause the bat to move a millimeter from the spot where the eyes say the ball is. Being still also helps concentration. Some batters like to *dance*, or move their feet around or shake the bat. It may help their nerves, but it never helps their swing. Batters should be still—coiled—waiting and ready to explode on the ball in one sharp, quick motion.

Learn what to look for in a stance. Look at the placement of the feet, the knees, the hands. Is the batter standing too stiffly? If so, suggest he bend his knees and waist to loosen up. Look at the swing. Is it level? Is he dropping his shoulder, elbow, hands, whole right side? Does he see the ball as it travels the entire way to the bat?

Talk about these ideas as you work with players. Tell them to stay balanced. Get them thinking about these things, not worrying how well they are doing. Get their minds off themselves and onto the ball. Remember, be still but not stiff! (See figure 2-4 on pages 26–27.)

Circle Stance Drill. A useful coaching tool is to get six players in a circle and have them get into the initial stance. The coach stands in the middle and calls out corrective instructions for each player. Each player gets to see the others' stances from various angles and learn from the coach's comments.

THE TOP EIGHT FUNDAMENTALS OF A GREAT SWING

We have touched on the initial stages of the swing, such as keeping the eye on the ball all the way to the bat; keeping loose but still; leaning forward with the weight back on the balls of the toes of the back foot; keeping the bat pointed up and back a bit; keeping the wrists and forearms strong; and holding the bat firmly, right elbow away from the body, hands up. Now we'll discuss the swing itself. Figure 2-5 on page 29 illustrates the four main stages of the swing.

1. Cock and load: the loaded stance. I think of this as baseball's version of the golf backswing, but very subtle. The weight shifts back a bit more, the front knee cocks in a

2-5. THE SWING

A: Loaded stance. Body cocks a bit, hands reach back slightly, weight on back foot, left shoulder tucked under chin.

B: Stride. Lift foot toward pitch, begin to shift weight forward, body still closed, eyes on the ball.

C: Drive. "Squash the bug," open hips, then open upper torso, keep head steady, extend arms, and move hands toward ball.

D: Follow through fully. Head and eyes still on the ball, chin goes from shoulder to shoulder.

02

bit, the front shoulder rotates in, and the hands reach back for more power. The whole body rotates back, just a tad, cocks, and loads up. In chapter nine, we'll review the science of plyometrics, which describes how muscles load up just before contracting; this is what happens in the loaded stance. Some batters hitch, lower, and raise the hands in an exaggerated cocking movement as they load. A big hitch takes time and may cause a player to swing late at a fastball. A key is to minimize the body movement to just a slight rotation. A good initial stance minimizes the amount of movement needed to get fully loaded. Cocking and loading are the first movements in the batter's swing.

Load-Up Drill. Have batters start in the initial stance, and at the coach's command, cock back and load, and hold the loaded stance. Have them think about the loaded stance, and feel where their bat, hand, elbow, hip, and knee positions are.

2. Look for a good pitch. Keep the eyes on the ball to be able to pick out a good pitch. I repeat often that "seeing the ball" is the most important hitting fundamental. As the pitcher is getting ready to throw, yell out to your batter, "Get a fat one!" (in essence, see the whole ball). A ball outside of the strike zone usually cannot be hit well, nor can it be hit hard. High pitches pop up; low ones dive into the turf and become weak grounders. Inside or outside pitches are usually hit foul. Tell your batter to look for the good pitch. Tell him to never let a good pitch go by because you don't get that many. When you pitch, talk about each pitch—"Was that a ball or a strike?" During practices, it's okay to swing at bad pitches (if they are at least close!) because it teaches bat control, but make sure the batter knows when the pitch is not in the strike zone. Eventually, he will be able to tell the difference before the ball is halfway to him. Talk about these concepts.

3. Stride into the pitch. The next part of the swing is called the *stride*. It is a very short 4- to 6-inch step (maybe a bit more for older kids) made directly toward the pitcher. Often, the stride is even shorter, just a brief lifting of the front foot. The idea is to get the body moving, turning into the ball. The lifting of the front foot is the first action after loading the stance. The batter should keep the weight on the back foot for as long as possible to prevent striding too soon or lunging at the ball.

The problem with getting a good stride is that the second biggest fear of younger kids in batting is getting hit by the ball. (The biggest is fear of embarrassing themselves.) A major problem with many kids is what we call "stepping into the bucket." (See figure 2-6 A on page 32.) They step away from the ball, toward third base, as they swing. This causes their body, and consequently the bat, to move out of the strike zone. No way can they hit anything, except maybe an inside pitch.

I remember a husky, freckle-faced redheaded ten year old who had a bad habit of stepping into the bucket. His dad said he had been doing it for two years. He was a good hitter, except he usually couldn't reach the ball after stepping back so far, and he struck out a lot. I had his father put a piece of wood (4x4) behind his feet in practice, and it worked. (Using a bat behind the feet will also work.) It took a while, but he settled down and started to reach his full potential as a hitter.

Some kids don't stride at all. Their swing is stiff and jerky, making it very hard to hit the ball squarely. (See figure 2-6 B on page 32).

Fifty Strides Drill. Have your players take practice swings, without a pitched ball. Just drive and swing, about fifty times a day. Tell them to pretend they see the ball coming toward them and to stride into the pitch and swing. It will loosen up their swing. Don't let them get sloppy. Do about twenty-five at first and build up to fifty quality swings. If it gets to be a habit, they will do it naturally in a real situation. My kids and I used to swing a bat in the living room, talking about the stance and the swing. Try it, but move the lamps out of the way.

4. The drive. Now your player is ready to begin the swing, which is a quick, powerful, balanced, exploding action. He must drive or push himself forward with the inside pads and toes of the back foot. The back foot pivots, drives into the ground ("squashing the bug") as the back knee turns in, allowing first the hips and then the whole upper torso to turn. Note that the turn of the hips must precede and lead the shoulder turn. The rear hip explodes toward the ball, delivering the power from the legs to the upper torso. The left foot strides, as reviewed above, and then pivots upon the heel. *The head remains steady* throughout the swing, chin riding from shoulder to shoulder. Players should not just push off the back foot, but roll forward on the inside edge. This curl will bring the back knee in and turn the hips out—good for generating bat speed at the plate.

Remember, the idea is to get the body moving with the swing into the ball and to avoid stepping away from the ball. Avoid lunging at the ball, which occurs when the shoulders and arms lead the swing, instead of drawing power from the torque of the opening hips. (See figure 2-6 C on page 32.)

5. Open the hips. As noted earlier, the batter should keep the weight back and hips steady for as long as possible. Then, just at the end of the stride and the beginning of the swing, the hips turn or *open up*, giving power, speed, and torque to the swing. The hips ultimately open up completely, facing the pitcher. It's important to teach kids to turn the hips, since driving the hips forward without a turn will cause the back shoulder to drop. You will see this very often. Look for it and fix it.

2-6. **IMPROPER SWINGS**

A: "Stepping into the bucket"—front leg steps toward third base, pulls head and bat away.

B: Too stiff, no stride, hips not open.

C: Lunge—reaching for the ball too soon.

D: Uppercut swing—hips move to ball, shoulders tilt, head comes up.

But make sure batters don't open too soon. Opening the hips and shoulders too soon will cause the batter's whole body, including the head and eyes, to pull off the pitch. This flaw often causes the barrel of the bat to lag and reduces bat speed. Much less plate coverage is possible.

A good concept in teaching hip movement is to relate the hands to the belly. Have the batter try to keep the belly even with the hands during the swing, rotating the belly along with the hands.

6. Thrust the hands at the ball. The hands are thrust toward the ball. A tight, choppy swing, with the hands close to the chest, often goes along with stepping into the bucket. It's a defensive swing. Such a swing may suggest some self-doubt or concern about getting hit by the ball. It's often found with a stance that puts the weight back on the heels, standing straight up instead of leaning forward at the knees and waist. On the other hand, we don't want the arms extended stiffly, and certainly not extended too soon. The arms extend slowly through the swing, hands moving not "out," but toward the ball. The arms are comfortably, but not stiffly, extended at point of contact.

7. Swing level, but at the ball. The way to teach kids to swing level is to tell them to straighten out the left arm and to move the hands directly toward the ball on a straight line. Perceive the bat coming down to meet the ball rather than coming up into it. The bat will then also move on a straight line. As noted earlier, holding the hands up and keeping the shoulders level (don't drop the right side) also help make a level swing.

I remember a nine year old who loved to play ball and did it with his heart. But he had the worst swing I ever saw. It looked like he was hitting a golf ball out of a sand trap, with a wild, looping uppercut. First, if he hit the ball, it went straight up. Second, he missed a lot because such a swing requires great timing. The bat is moving upward and has to meet the ball at a single spot. A level swing can meet the ball anywhere over the plate. Third, such a swing causes the shoulders to tilt severely, and this moves the head up and takes the eyes off the ball. (See figure 2-6 D on page 32.)

I tried everything with this player. I had him hold his hands higher and keep his right elbow up more. His problem was that he lifted the front elbow and shoulder and dropped the right side. Then, I told him to try to chop down at the ball, like chopping down a tree. (By the way, these suggestions usually do work, and you should always try them first.) Finally, I had no choice but to tell him to bat lefty. Kids usually will swing level from the opposite side, but with less power. He hit the ball well. The next year, his coach moved him back to righty, and by then, time had softened the arc in his swing. Some things just need time.

Another problem behind an uppercut swing is that the batter lifts up the head, trying to add more power. If this occurs, remind your player to keep the head down and still. I saw a coach recently put a glove on his batter's head to keep the head from jerking out. The batter learned to keep the head still or the glove would drop before contact.

8. Follow through. Some kids just chop or slap at the ball. Batters need to follow through with the swing, so that the bat ends up all the way around and behind them. The idea is to flick the wrists and hit *through* the ball. Batters should hold the head down as long as possible, and keep the back foot down, on the toes, but not dragging.

BATTING PRACTICE DRILLS AND TIPS

No-Pitch Drill. Probably the best way to coach the techniques for a proper swing is to have the player hit off a batting tee, or to use the No-Pitch Drill. In this drill, the coach or parent lobs the ball into the strike zone from a spot about 6 feet from the plate, off to the side of the batter. (See figure 2-7.) The drill can be done on the open field, but is far better if done in a cage or into a net, saving time rounding up balls. The idea is to make a lot of swings and have the coach carefully observe each part of the swing, especially the hip opening, the head position, the arm extension, and the swing plane. Only work on one of these areas at a time: stride, drive, hips, arm extension, head down,

2-7. **NO-PITCH DRILL**

Lob ball from the side from about 6 feet away.

and follow through. Occasionally, lob two balls at the same time and call out which one, high or low, should be hit. The pros hit off batting tees every day, and if it's good for them, it's good for youth players. There are also a number of gadgets on the market that allow for swing practice; for example, long rubber poles with a ball on the end.

Golf Balls Drill. Get a bunch of plastic practice golf balls (they're lightweight, hollow balls) and throw them to batters from 6 to 10 feet away. Sit in a chair or throw from a knee so that they come in level. This is great for getting the kids to focus on the ball. Have them try to hit to different sides of the field.

Pitch-on-One-Knee Drill. Here is another one of my secrets, maybe my best one! When I pitched to my kids, I did so while down on my right knee. (See figure 2-8.) I've been doing it this way for many, many years. I remember when I was a kid, my coach always seemed so tall, and the ball would be coming down on me from 8 feet high. It would be dropping fast, and I had to swing an uppercut to get solid contact. When you pitch on a knee, the ball leaves your hand at the same height that a ten-year-old's pitch leaves his hand. It comes to the batter in a much more level flight.

Now, pitching from the knee might sound tough, and it can be awkward, but you will get used to it. If the players are young, and you do it from 35 to 40 feet, you can develop some control. You have to have faith in practice if you are going to teach its value to someone else! If your players are older, around eleven or twelve, don't get closer than 40 feet or you might wind up eating the ball.

2–8. **PITCHING ON ONE KNEE**

The best tip I have! An adult's pitch comes in lower and more level. (That's me with my wife and son.)

By the way, you don't need a catcher, just a backstop. And don't let another player or adult get behind the batter without a face mask and other protection. A foul tip is hard to catch and may hit the face. You'll get used to the strike zone. If you have several balls, use them all, then go pick them up, or have an on-deck hitter and the batter pick them up. This allows for many swings in a short period. I use about ten or fifteen balls. I buy a box of twelve each year for myself. If your kid is under ten, the cheap cork balls are good enough. However, older kids bang them out of shape too quickly. One more tip: Get something soft to kneel on—it will be easier to be able to walk after practice. I used a catcher's chest protector. A small pillow also works.

I think pitching on my knee has resulted in quality batting practices. My teams always hit the ball, so something is working.

Other Drills. There are two other drills that are good, especially for parents who want to work one-on-one with their child and want to save time chasing after balls. Your local sporting goods store will have a "ball on a string" that you whip around your head in a circular motion as you step toward your child, moving the ball into the strike zone. This is excellent practice for seeing the ball. A better drill is to stand to the side and lob the ball into the strike zone while the batter stands facing the backstop (or a net), so the ball doesn't travel far. Have him work on his stance and hitting down on the ball—no pop-ups allowed.

Have you ever heard of "pepper"? It's a fielding exercise they do in the big leagues. A coach stands 6 feet from a couple of players and softly hits them grounders. Players lob the ball back to the bat and the coach hits it to someone else; you keep it moving and it develops reflexes. I do the reverse for batting. I get the kids up close with bats and they try to softly tap the ball to where I tell them—at my shoe, my knee, my glove. It's a great drill that builds confidence and a sense of contact with the ball.

EQUIPMENT

A few words about equipment are in order. Little League starts in the spring, and it's often cold. When it's cold, the bat stings the hands upon contact with the ball. A batting glove will eliminate the sting. Get one for each hand; cheap ones will do. If the player's winter gloves are not too thick, they will work, too. Even a pair of socks are better than nothing, although they will make the bat a bit slippery and harder to hold onto. Helmets are a must: any hard hat or helmet will do.

Spikes help give traction to the right foot as it drives the body toward the ball, but they are not essential for practice.

BUYING A BAT

Bats can range from under twenty dollars to over three hundred dollars. Remember, use a light bat; don't fall into the trap of getting something so heavy it warps the swing. Bats made of aluminum are fairly inexpensive, but are significantly heavier than some modern alloy bats. Since bat speed is crucial to generating power, heavier bats can be counter-productive. At beginner levels, the bats supplied by the team are fine, and personal bats are quite unnecessary. If at some point you choose to buy your child his own bat, as a rule of thumb buy the lightest bat of a given length that you can afford. It's all about the thickness of the walls of the bat, since performance is much higher with thinner walls. The high-tech but expensive alloys allow the aluminum to be thinned and still preserve strength. Bats have a length-to-weight factor, a negative number that subtracts the length from the weight. Thus a 28-inch bat that weighs 18 ounces has a -10 factor.

Most beginners who are 4 feet to 5 feet in height should use a bat between 16 and 19 ounces, and 29 to 32 inches in length. Have your child hold a potential bat straight out sideways, fully extending his arm. If he can't hold it for twenty seconds, it's too heavy. A kid who weighs between 100 and 150 pounds should use a bat that weighs from 20 to 23 ounces; and if he's over 5 feet tall, he should get a bat that is 32 to 34 inches in length. By high school or college, bats are from 27 to 30 ounces and from 33 to 35 inches in length; the numbers are even higher in the pros. Little League rules require the bat barrel to have a diameter no greater than 2¼ inches.

SWITCH-HITTING

Not too many kids can switch hit. It's tough enough to get good from one side of the plate. When you watch the pros, the team is platooned—righties face only lefty pitchers, and vice versa. The idea is that a right-handed batter can see the ball better if it comes from the *outside*, that is, from the pitcher's left side. It starts out in front of the batter. However, if a pitcher is a righty, especially a sidearm righty, the ball seems like it's starting from behind the batter. So, switch-hitters have the advantage of always seeing the pitch from the outside. I really can't say I've emphasized switch-hitting. I do have my kids bat lefty for a few pitches at practices just so they can experience what it feels like. I basically use the switched stance to give a slightly different perspective to a kid and to change something a player is doing wrong.

When I was eight years old, we moved from Jersey City to "the country," and I had never played baseball. I joined a team and couldn't hit the ball to save my life. Then one day, after what seemed like a million strikeouts, my coach told me to get up lefty. I don't know whether he had an idea or was just frustrated. But I got a hit the first time up. The new angle forced me to look at the ball differently, and somehow I saw it better (maybe because the pitcher was a righty). I also swung more level. It felt awkward, and I had less power, but it worked. After a while, I returned to righty and became a power hitter. Make sure you give your players the chance to hit from the other side of the plate at least during practices.

BUNTING

Bunting is a lost art in youth baseball. Very few coaches teach it because the pitcher is so close to the batter (only 46 feet instead of 60 feet 6 inches as in the pros), and he can retrieve the ball very quickly and throw the batter out. Nevertheless, it should be practiced.

I remember a playoff game in 1986 for nine year olds where we needed a run to tie the score. We were facing the best pitcher in the league. He threw hard, and he threw strikes. The boy who was up could make contact, but he was small and couldn't get the ball out of the infield, not against that pitcher. The *on-deck batter* (the next batter up) was a very good hitter. So I told the batter to bunt and run like the dickens. It worked. He got on base, and my next batter tied the game with a shot into the gap. It was a good thing we had practiced bunting the night before!

When practicing bunting, tell the batter to turn and face the pitcher just as he pitches the ball. (See figure 2-9 on page 39.) This can be done by fully turning the body, or just by opening the hips and bending the knees. The batter should slide his right hand a third of the way toward the top of the bat, keeping the head of the bat high in the strike zone. The goal is to hit the top half of the ball. I also tell older players to slide the lower hand along the bat a bit toward the middle. It makes the bat more flexible, but younger players may not be able to control the bat's recoil. When bunting, a player must concentrate on the ball more closely and watch its spin, then let the *ball* hit the *bat*. If the batter moves the bat toward the ball, the ball will roll right to the pitcher; so, he must hold the bat firmly and just "catch the pitch," letting the ball hit the bat, even recoiling the head of the bat back a bit. Tell your player to picture a glove on the bat, as if he is trying to catch the ball. Then, he should try to push the ball down the third base line softly and, upon contact, push off his back foot to begin running to first base. Foot speed helps here. Tell your players to not look back, just go for the base.

OTHER TIPS

If you have read this far, you know as much as you need to know about hitting to help your players. Let's summarize, and if this seems repetitious, then I'm practicing what I preach, and I'll do a lot of repetition in this book.

Turn to face the pitcher, feet balanced, head of bat up a bit. Cradle mid-bat between thumb and forefinger, with a soft touch. Bottom hand can choke up quite a ways for more control.

• **Be supportive generally.** Get your child to practice on time, or help arrange for someone else to bring him. If you are a coach and a kid has problems getting to practice that his parent can't or won't resolve, ask if a player nearby can pick him up.

• **Be positive.** He is a hitter already, he just has to believe it. Don't help him confirm doubts about himself.

• **Promote repetition.** Tell parents to go out and pitch to their kids, or have a catch. If there are a few kids around, suggest they play ball. Get them organized into a game, help oversee it, and pitch to them. Sometimes kids will argue for two hours about who is on which team or who is up first. You can help get them beyond that and get them on their way to playing. When I pitched to my son Joey, I would grab a bucket of balls and it took only about ten or fifteen minutes to make thirty to forty swings. We picked up the balls together.

Well, that's it for hitting. Even if you only improve hitting, you'll be a great help, because hitting is of primary importance. However, if you want your players to be really good at the other things they do while they are waiting to bat, then read on!

03

FIELDING

The old joke is that defense is just "de thing you try to hit de ball over." Well, it's true that hitting is the glory of baseball, but teams rarely win without good defense. Unfortunately, defense is often the last thing kids learn. Many youth coaches just hit a few grounders to kids and have outfielders catch fly balls, and not many know how to teach the basics. I'm not being critical of youth coaches, it's just that defense is a stepchild skill of this great game, and little quality time is spent on it at young ages. Coaches often figure a kid either has defensive skills or he doesn't.

As a result, a typical youth baseball scenario starts with what should be an "easy out" ground ball, and pretty soon, instead of that easy out, players are throwing the ball all over the place. Scores are high with the younger kids because of poor defense.

Part of the problem is that there is never enough practice time. You get the kids for only a few hours a week, if you're lucky. During the season, the well-groomed club fields are often reserved for games, so there is very little practice opportunity. Neighborhood fields are sometimes badly rutted, especially in early springtime, and not good for defensive practice. That is where parents come in. As a coach, I spend a lot of time talking to parents about how to help their children play better defense. Parents often want to help—they just need some good ideas on how to do so. Substantial improvement in defensive play can come with regular practice in the backyard or on a side street.

Fielding is essentially catching and throwing, and knowing where to throw. I'll address these skills generally. Chapter five also discusses defense, but from the perspective of each field position.

CATCHING BALLS

The best way to learn how to catch, particularly at very young ages, is to do just that—have a catch. Every practice should begin with the kids having a catch to loosen

3-1. HAVE A CATCH

Perhaps the easiest and most effective form of practice ... Play catch!

up. Except at beginner levels, you can't afford to waste too much time on this during practices because there are so many other skills kids need to learn. Tell parents to get a couple of gloves and a ball and go outside with their child for a catch. This is important for kids who don't catch well.

At first, throw the ball softly back and forth. Start at a comfortable distance. For beginners, throw underhanded from 8 to 10 feet. (See figure 3-1.) As soon as the kid can handle it, throw overhanded from 15 to 25 feet, and then go back farther, up to 60 feet when he is ready. I've seen many parents learn how to do this very quickly, especially mothers who have had little or no experience with baseball. Remember, if *you* practice, you will improve, too, so don't be bashful. It may be easier to use a tennis ball at first, or, even better, a rubber ball with a sponge-like filling. A rubber ball weighs a bit more, behaving like a hard ball in flight, but it won't hurt if it hits you. I frequently use a rubber ball when I have outfield practice, especially for young players who have trouble catching. Go to a hard ball when you can.

Remember, the key to building confidence is not pushing too hard. If it's not working, don't get angry. Start from a position that allows the player to do well, and gradually increase the difficulty. The primary goal is steady improvement. Recognize and celebrate improvement. If you start with too difficult a distance, the child will only learn to fail. If it's not working, make it easier. A challenge is okay, but an impossible challenge is only a negative experience.

THE FIVE KEYS TO CATCHING FLY BALLS

Catching fly balls is not difficult, but it is one of the last things kids learn to do well.

1. Get under the ball. The main idea in catching pop-ups is to get under the ball so it's traveling right at the head. I know this sounds strange, but it's the best way

3-2. CATCHING FLY BALLS

Proper position—directly under the ball, glove high, palm outward, free hand up and ready to trap the ball.

3-3. CHASING DOWN POP-UPS

On a deep fly ball, do not backpedal. Turn and run back to get under it.

to catch. It's just like hitting: You must keep your eye on the ball, and you can see it best when it's coming right at your eyes. The glove should be above the head when catching the ball, fingers up, palm outward. The tip of the glove is just below the line between the ball and the eyes, ready to snatch the ball just as it approaches the player. (See figure 3-2.)

Many kids are afraid to try this for obvious reasons, especially if they have already been hit by a ball. So they let the ball fall to one side of them and try to catch it at the waist. Now they have to calculate two more angles, and it's much easier to misjudge. If the ball is coming right at the eye, all the player has to do is stick his glove in the way at the right time. This is why I use rubber or tennis balls for beginners. They know it won't hurt since it's rubber, so they will try harder to get under it. Take it slow, start with a short distance if you need to, and, over a few weeks, work out to a longer distance. Pick an appropriate angle so the sun is not in their eyes. Build confidence slowly. It may take a very long time, so just relax and be patient.

2. Stay back. Kids usually misjudge fly balls by coming in too far and letting the ball go over their heads. So when your child shows that he can catch the ball, start to vary the distance. First throw over his head. Then throw one short. On line drives to the right of the fielder, he will have to turn his glove backward and catch it backhanded. On throws over his head, tell him to turn and run, not just backpedal! (See figure 3-3.) He will get to the ball faster and can make a more relaxed catch.

3. Run laterally as quickly as possible. The key to catching outfield pop-ups is to run laterally very quickly to where the ball will land. It's far better to get there quickly, and have time to catch the ball while under it, than to catch it on the run, stretched out. When practicing, hit or throw the ball to either side and make sure kids understand how much easier it is to catch when they get there quickly. Of course, part of lateral quickness is being ready when the ball is hit and not getting off to a slow start. Many more balls get caught with a quick first step.

4. Use two hands. Remind players to try to catch the ball in the webbing of the glove, between the thumb and index finger. This reduces the chance that the ball will pop out, and it avoids stinging the palm of the hand. Also, tell the fielder to use both hands. The free hand stays by the glove and smothers the ball when it hits the glove. This accomplishes two things: It keeps the ball from popping out of the glove, and it gets the ball into the throwing hand faster so the fielder wastes no time getting the ball back to the infield.

5. Fungo practice. This involves a coach hitting the ball to the fielders, either infield or outfield. The coach uses a *fungo bat,* which is a long, thin, lightweight bat designed for this purpose. It takes some skill to do. That is why fungo bats are extra big. For young players, I find it more effective to throw the ball to them. You may, too! Don't throw your arm out. Always warm up first with a dozen or so short throws, and then go for some long ones. Just get a dozen or so long ones in; that's all each player needs at each session.

It's good to move to different drills, just a few minutes on each. Variety keeps everyone more interested. Focus on different skills each day.

It may be that a child will miss nearly every catch at first. "No problem," tell him. "Tomorrow or the next day we'll catch one or two. Then after that more." Focus on slight improvement. Don't set expectations too high. Don't get frustrated—your player will sense your frustration and feel it too. After a while, he will improve.

TOP SEVEN KEYS TO CATCHING GROUNDERS

I think catching infield grounders is the toughest thing in youth baseball. It takes a quick reflex, speed, and good concentration to be an infielder. Again, some people figure that you either have it or you don't. This is not true; fielding can be learned.

Eye-hand coordination varies for kids. It can be tested. Chapter nine discusses how to improve vision and coordination. It's true that everybody can't play everywhere, and at advanced levels this is certainly the case. But at beginner- and even intermediate-level play, give each kid a shot at playing infield. Coaches tend to quickly pick the best infielder early, and the other kids don't see a grounder for the rest of the season. Don't let this happen at early ages.

The first thing is to find a smooth surface. Most grass fields are terrible. They teach a kid to fear grounders since bad hops occur very frequently. A dirt field is much better, and you can rake out any ruts and remove stones. I often took my son to a parking lot. City parents can use a side street if traffic is very light. Throw the ball sidearm to make sure you release it about 2 feet from the ground—the height where a bat would hit it. At first, let the fielder stand fairly close, and throw the ball softly, getting it to him on one bounce. Again, throwing the ball works as well as hitting it and takes less skill on your part. Also, you can put the ball exactly where you want it. After a while, when he can handle it, make it tougher. Give a couple of bounces, vary the speed, throw to the right or left. As in the outfield, the fielder reverses the glove position on shots to the side opposite the glove hand, catching it backhanded. After skills are improved, move onto a regular infield and use a bat to hit the balls to him.

For beginners, visual concepts work well. Tell them their hands are like a great jaw, with the glove as the bottom jaw and the throwing hand as the top jaw. Open and close the jaws like a big alligator, scooping up the ball. A popular concept at the intermediate level is the funnel, with the lower legs and shoulders as the open end of the funnel and the glove as the recipient.

1. Ready and waiting. Kids are kids, and so a significant problem in youth ball is that players don't focus, and usually are not ready for the ball. They stand up, daydream, and as a result get off to a slow start when the ball is hit near them. The players must be instructed to get into ready stance (see number three below) with each pitch, and to anticipate, even hope, that the ball is hit to them. It's good to teach them to take one or two short or stutter steps with the pitch, so they are loose and in motion as the ball is hit.

2. See the ball. As with hitting, the essential factor in catching grounders is to see the ball, concentrate on it, and try to see it spin. During practice, yell this out constantly to kids until it becomes second nature. Looking at or toward a ball does not mean you see it with sufficient focus to catch it. Talk to the players about the difference between looking and seeing. Throw some one-hop, short grounders and have them think about seeing the ball fully.

3. Stance. The player initially stands in a crouch, facing the batter, legs spread out a bit, knees and hips bent, hands and gloves down by the knees, weight forward on the toes so he can spring either way to field the ball. As noted, and worth repeating, many infielders get themselves moving a bit toward the batter with the pitch, so the muscles are in motion, ready to spring. (See figure 3-4, step one, on page 46.)

4. Step to the ball. The first movement in fielding a grounder is to step towards the ball. Also, as with fly balls, the idea is to very quickly get in front of the ball so it's coming right at you. When the ball is hit, the player *springs* to get quickly to the spot where he can make the play. When moving to the right, step out with the right foot and drive off the left foot, driving and turning the left hip and left shoulder towards the right. Similarly, to move left, step with the left foot and drive with the right foot.

5. Stand up and sit down. I used to tell my players that infielders have to "stand up and sit down at the same time." The legs are spread apart, left foot up, right foot back. The knees are bent so the backside is down low. (Not really sitting of course, but it makes the point. We want the body low.) Most players prefer to bend over at the waist; a waist bend is needed but not at the expense of bending the knees. The back is down nearly parallel to the ground, but the head is up and the eyes are on the ball. "Bend at the knees, not from the waist." Repeat this sentence constantly. (See figure 3-4, step two, on page 46.)

6. Two hands. A critical element of good fielding in any position is to use both hands to trap the ball in the glove. It also hastens the transition of the ball from the glove to the throwing hand.

7. Glove low. The glove should be down below the ball. "Come up with some dirt on it," I always say. Honus Wagner used to throw a handful of dirt with the ball. If the ball goes under the glove, it's all over. Start the glove low, and bring it forward and up to meet the ball. Visualize a triangle formed by the glove and both feet. Players often expect the ball to bounce up to them, but sometimes it doesn't. If the bat hit the top of the ball, the topspin will make the ball skim the ground. The glove must always be low in anticipation. If the ball skims, it's easier to bring the glove up to meet it than down.

Another popular tip, noted earlier, is to tell your infielders to visualize a funnel with the open mouth receiving the ball and channeling or funneling it up to the waist. A key here is that the hands must be soft, giving way to the ball. The scooping action brings the glove forward to the ball, then gently back to the waist. (See figure 3-4, step three, on page 46.) Tell them to think of their hands as soft.

3-4. **FIELDING GROUNDERS**

Step 1: Proper stance as ball is pitched. Body low, knees bent, waist bent, balanced glove down and out, head up, poised.

Step 2: Stand up and sit down: Get low, bend knees, and lower glove.

Step 3: Keep head down and scoop the ball up and back to the waist.

Step 4: Once ball is under control, come up ready to fire.

Tell fielders that it's important not to stand back on the heels, just waiting for the ball. A fielder must play the ball. If the ball is slow, run to get it; otherwise get in front of it and scoop it up. Forward action is the aggressiveness needed to command the ball. Again, if you practice on a smooth surface, these skills will be much easier to demonstrate and learn.

The biggest problems with kids catching grounders are (1) not getting in front of the ball; (2) using only one hand; (3) not getting the glove low enough (not bending the knees enough); (4) catching the ball too close to the body; and (5) coming up too soon, especially with the head, which I'll explain next.

I had an all-star first baseman in 1987, a ten year old named Chris. He could hit the ball a mile, but his fielding was not consistent. One day before regular practice, he and his father got there early to practice grounders. He had made some errors the previous game, and I was a bit worried. I guess they were, too. I watched him closely, focusing on different parts of his body. After several plays, I saw it! Just as the ball was about to be caught, he would lift up his head, and then his shoulders would follow, then his arms, and of course, finally, his glove. It's understandable. Kids are worried about the ball getting a bad hop into the face, so they lift or turn their heads. I told Chris about it, and then kept saying, "Stay down, stay down, stay calm" as the ball approached him. It took a while, but he started to adjust. As I've said before, a coach needs to study his players and to look at each part of their forms. In this way, problems will be seen.

Rapid-Fire Drill. Reflexes are important in infield play. You must practice them. I used to get two balls and stand about 20 feet from my son. I would throw one, then throw the other one just as he was releasing the first ball back to me. Quick, to the left, to the right, changing speeds. It improves the reflexes. That is another drill you can do for a few minutes each session.

Remember, as with hitting, don't be impatient with the misses and the errors (also call "booted balls"). They happen even to the pros. Reward the catches with a smile, or "Way to go." And repeat, repeat, repeat! Repetition is the backbone of success and improvement. The more the better.

Bat Drill. Young players make the mistake of letting ground balls get too close to their body before catching them. They need to make sure to field the ball in front of them. Place a bat on the ground at the shortstop position, and another at second base. Line up players behind each bat. Hit a ball, and have the player charge up and field the ball. He must not let the ball hit the bat, and he cannot step over the bat to field the ball. In other words, he must field the ball out in front of the bat. Alternate hits between the two bats.

Goalie Grounder Drill. Put two empty bottles a short distance to the left and right, like a soccer goal, and see how many grounders your player can stop. Keep score, have a goal. Increase it over time. Tell him constantly to keep his eye on the ball. (See figure 3-5 on page 48.)

3-5. **GOALIE GROUNDER DRILL**

Set up cones as goalposts on sand or soft grass and have fielder try to stop grounders.

THE GLOVE

The glove may be the most important thing in catching. Each child needs a decent glove, and it must be broken in, or softened up. It is nearly impossible to catch a ball with the cheap, rigid, plastic gloves you find in a toy store. The ball will just jump out every time. Even a good glove takes a while to break in.

When I get a new glove, I literally beat it up. I rub glove oil into it and bend every inch of it back and forth. Shaving cream with lanoline also works well. Keep bending the fingers back and forth. Years ago, players used to drop a new glove in a pail of water and hang it out to dry (I've never tried it, but it sounds bizarre!). The point is that the glove should be soft enough to collapse on the ball. I've seen so many kids get a negative picture of their ability because of the cheap, stiff gloves they have. Some modern gloves are pre-oiled and are more supple than ones from the past, so look for these when you buy a glove. Gloves with some vinyl are also softer, but don't last as long as all-leather gloves. Nonetheless, they are fine for beginners, who will grow out of their gloves after a season or two anyway.

When practice is over, leave a ball in the pocket of the glove and wrap the glove around it. In the off-season, wrap tape around the glove to keep the ball in place. Oiling once or twice a season is sufficient.

Gloves today seem oversized, and at the beginner level it's better to have a glove that is comfortable than a glove that is too large. It needs to be able to be controlled to move quickly to the ball and quickly collapse around the ball.

In addition to regular gloves, there are first baseman's and catcher's mitts. Specialty gloves will be supplied by the team. Beginners don't specialize enough to warrant owning one at beginner levels. By nine or ten years old, it may be that such specialty has become evident, and so a personal glove may be useful.

THROWING

There is really not a lot of science about throwing. (Pitching yes, throwing no.) But there is a lot you can do to practice it. Throwing is almost totally dependent on just doing it. Each player needs to throw the ball a few thousand times to get the smooth style of a decent throw. Suggest to parents that they regularly have a catch with their child. It's something you can do anywhere, anytime. Having a catch at early ages is critical for developing a good throw.

Start nice and easy, at a comfortable distance, and slowly move back, up to 60 feet for older kids. The more times your child throws the ball, the faster and better his arm will work out the coordination needed.

TOP NINE THROWING BASICS

Of course, there are a few basics you can look for.

1. Get balanced. Once a player catches a ball, it's important to get the feet back under the body. Sometimes this takes a hop to get into position.

2. Grip. The proper grip on the ball is very standard—thumb on bottom, the next two fingers (index and middle) on top, the last two fingers tucked on the side. If the

3-6. GRIPPING THE BALL

A: Proper grip. Ball not set too deeply into hand.

B: If the hand is small, all three middle fingers may be placed on top.

49

player's hand is small, let him use the three middle fingers on top, with only the pinky tucked on the side. Fingers can straddle or cross the seams, but in a fielding play, he won't have time to worry about seams. Also, make sure the ball is not set back in the hand too far—there should be some space between the palm and the ball. The idea is to throw with the fingers. (See figure 3-6 on page 49.)

3. Align with the target. This is important. At the beginning of the throw, the body is sideways to the target. The shoulder, elbow, and foot nearest the target point right at it. The throwing hand reaches back and upward, directly opposite the target. The front foot lifts and strides toward the target. (See figure 3-7.)

4. Crow hop. It helps velocity to make one hop, or a shuffling move, on the back foot just before driving with that foot.

5. Plant and drive. Players should plant and drive the back foot toward the target. Often kids will drive or push off the wrong foot. To be a coaching parent, you must force yourself to focus on different parts of the body, to find things the player is doing wrong. I recall such a player: When I looked at the foot position, I saw him throwing off the left foot. That is, he was pushing off the left foot and stepping forward with the right foot—it was backwards! The idea in throwing (for righties) is to step with the left foot and push off with the right foot as you begin the throw, landing on the left as you release the throw. When the fielder is ready to throw, he should stand a bit sideways, point the left shoulder at the target, reach back with the ball, and then step and drive off the back foot, even rolling it a bit along the edge from instep to toe.

3-7. THROWING FORM

Proper form. Pushing off same foot as throwing arm (right arm, right foot). The other elbow, shoulder, and foot point to the target.

Sometimes there is no time to get set, and a fielder has to throw off balance or on the run. That's when many throwing errors are made.

6. Extend the arm. After reaching back with the ball with the throwing hand and elbow up, cock the arm and wrist to throw, and extend the arm. The idea is not to extend stiffly, but with power.

Many kids are "arm-throwers." They bend their elbows too much and throw entirely with their arms—it looks like they are literally "throwing the arm" instead of the ball. The cure is to ensure that the arm extends as it reaches back before the throw. Often, an arm-thrower does not reach back, because he begins the throw with the elbow bent too much. Another technique is to have the player go through the throwing motion without any shoulder action at all, just flicking the arm, without a ball. Then he can try it by stiffening the upper arm and throwing only with the shoulder. He should do this several times to get the feel of the shoulder's role in the throw. Actually, a good throw has every body part involved: toes, knees, hips, shoulder, elbow, and wrist.

When the arm is extended, the shoulder becomes the fulcrum, and it brings the strength of the entire body into the throw. The hands and arm move in a circular motion. The bent-elbow arm-thrower cuts off the power coming from the right leg, right hip, and right shoulder. He gets less power on the throw, and his arm will quickly tire since it is doing all the work. Remember to have players keep the elbow high—at or above the shoulder.

7. Rotate. Turn the shoulders, rotating the body, opening the hips, as the throwing arm comes forward. The body drives forward, and rotating snaps the throwing arm and shoulder down.

8. Don't aim. Never use the word *aim*. Aim means to guide the ball, and this removes power and velocity. You throw to a player, or to a glove, but accuracy and ball location ultimately come from repetition and good form. Eyes must look right at the target. Some kids like to throw the ball high in a big, soft arc. I think it's because they feel they control it better, or maybe it's because it's easier. However, high throws take more time to get to the infield. The ball should be released in front of the body simultaneously with a downward snap of the forearm.

9. Velocity. A long throw should be as hard and level as possible. A ball thrown straight on a line is called a *rope*. I always tell my players to throw right at the other kid's chest or head. It's the best height to catch the ball, so it's where the thrower should throw

51

it. For infielders, the key is to get the ball out of the glove as quickly as possible. The throwing hand should go for the ball the moment it hits the glove and make the transition very quickly.

Of course, the velocity of the throw depends on the position the fielder is playing. A third baseman or shortstop really has to rifle the ball to get it to first base. However, a second baseman only needs to ensure a firm throw to first base. If he throws too hard, he risks a control problem, like throwing the ball away, and it's also much harder for the first baseman to make the catch. A pitcher throwing to first base will often throw under-handed as he runs toward first with the ball. The shortstop will also make a softer throw to second base on a ball hit to his left side with a runner on first. The shortstop should field the ball, turn to the bag, and just lob the ball underhanded if he is very close to the second baseman. On grounders, the first baseman will softly lob the ball to the pitcher covering first base, if necessary. An outfielder, on the other hand, always throws hard.

The key to most throws is to get rid of the ball quickly. Far too often outfielders stand and hold the ball while runners are flying around the bases. They should use a quick shovel toss around any nearby infield bag, holding the ball out so the base-man sees a lot of white. They should stiffen the throwing arm and wrist a bit and aim at the glove.

Target Practice Drill. Have the kids line up at shortstop to first base distance. Hit or throw a grounder, and have the player try to hit a target. A five-gallon bucket, or an old tire mounted on a chair, will do. This drill also works for outfield to second base distance throws.

THROWING AHEAD OF THE LEAD RUNNER AND HITTING THE CUTOFF

As noted earlier, in youth baseball, outfielders often hold the ball too long. Of course, the problem is that the kid often doesn't know where to throw the ball. He has to think about it, look at the runners, and decide where to throw. He sees a lot of commotion in the infield; he is excited because he just fielded a live ball, and he doesn't quite know what to do. So the runners run, and the parents scream, and the poor kid gets so nervous he throws the ball into the parking lot. Well, there is another way!

Outfielders should always be able to field the ball and come up throwing immediately and without hesitation. The way an outfielder should know ahead of time where to throw lies in two related concepts: throwing ahead of the lead runner and hitting the cutoff. The *lead runner* is the runner who is closest to scoring, and the first concept means simply that you try to stop that runner from advancing an additional base beyond the base he will already safely make. The outfielder should throw to that base—we'll call it the lead base—which is two bases from where the lead runner started. For instance, if the lead runner is on first base, we know he will safely advance to second base on a base hit, so the defense wants to hold him on second base and prevent him from getting to third base. Thus, the throw is to third base, two bases from where the runner starts.

The second concept, the *cutoff*, positions an infielder in line with, and well in front of, that lead base (third base in the example we just gave) in order to allow the defense the option of cutting off the throw and gaining more time to make a play against another runner. Which infielder is the cutoff depends on where the ball is hit and how many runners are on base. We'll review this in detail on pages 54–59.

Since this book is for youth coaches and parents, you may wonder whether I really need to go into detail on the difficult concept of the cutoff and lead runner. It is certainly a tough concept to master and takes precious practice time. At beginner levels, coaches are pressed just to get players to be able to hit and catch. I rarely see beginner or intermediate teams do much in this area. Many coaches don't understand the underlying concepts. Some just say, "Always throw the ball to second base." Well, I agree that it's better than nothing and better than holding the ball. But it's not good baseball. And a coach who doesn't understand the concept obviously can't teach it.

Actually, it's really very logical, commonsense stuff. I recommend at beginner-level play that you learn the concept of cutoff and then teach it to your players. It may take a whole season to get the hang of it, but it's part of the game. It will save runs on defense, and kids will need to learn it sometime. My suggestion is to spend some time on the concept at very young ages, but don't go crazy trying to get the kids to master it unless you practice a lot. Just tell them that they need to understand it and will be expected to perform it over time. In the meantime, be satisfied if they get the ball to second base. By the time they're ten to eleven years old, you can start pushing it.

WHO IS THE LEAD RUNNER?

Since this concept is based on the need to stop the lead runner, spend some time talking about who the lead runner is. As stated above, the lead runner is the one who is closest to scoring. If there are runners on first and second bases, the one on second is the lead runner. If there is only a runner on second, then he is obviously the lead runner. Particularly in such a situation, the infield players or coaches should remind the outfield players that the lead runner is in scoring position, since he could score on any base hit. Thus, the throw must be homeward, to the cutoff, who will line up with the outfield player and with home plate upon a base hit (we'll discuss cutoffs shortly).

If the only base runner is on first base, then he is the lead runner. He will easily get to second base on a hit, but he is the runner you want to stop from getting to third base. So, that's where the throw goes.

If no one is on base, the batter is by default the lead runner, and the goal is to prevent him from getting to second base.

A runner on third is never a lead runner, so forget about him on a base hit to the outfield. On a ball hit safely to the outfield, a runner on third will always score. Outfielders only worry about runners on first or second and the batter. The only time a runner on third comes into the picture for an outfielder is on a fly ball when the runner will tag up and try to go home.

To summarize, the way to stop the lead runner on a base hit is to throw two bases ahead of him. Players simply have to know where the lead runner is and throw to the lead base—which is two bases ahead of him. The outfielder must figure this out before the play starts, and then he will know where to throw on a base hit. When a ball is hit to him, he comes up throwing toward the lead base without hesitation.

THE CUTOFF

You now know who the lead runner is, and you know that on a base hit players have to throw the ball two bases from where that runner starts to prevent him from advancing into scoring position. There are three situations that now can arise that you need to consider. First, particularly for beginners, the outfielder may not be able to reach the lead base, especially on a throw home, or on a throw from right field to third base. Second, the throw may be errant or off line, and won't make it to the base. Third, the lead runner may have stopped at the prior base, but there may be a play against another runner. For instance, with the lead runner on second base and no one on first base, upon a base hit to the outfield, the outfielder should throw home. But if the lead runner stops at third, and the batter tries to get to second base on the throw home, he would ordinarily have ample time to do so. For all three situations, the defensive response is the cut-off play.

The cutoff infielder, lined up between the outfielder and the lead base (the target base), has the option of letting the ball go through to that base to make the play on the lead runner. He also has the option of catching it (cutting it off) if it's an off-line throw and then relaying it to the lead base. He can also cut it off to make a play on the batter or another runner. Sometimes there is simply no play needed and the ball should be cut off to get control of it.

Cutoff Positions

The cutoff player needs to line up between the outfielder and the base he will be throwing to. Let's review the various cutoff scenarios.

Bases empty. The simplest application of these concepts occurs when there is no one on base. In this situation, the batter is the lead runner. Therefore, since he will easily get to first base on a base hit, the throw from the outfield goes to second base, the lead base. So the adage we always hear at Little League games exhorting outfielders to get the ball to second base is actually correct, but only when there is no one on base. In this situation, the cutoff is the shortstop or second baseman depending on where the ball is hit. On a base hit to the right side of the field, or up the middle, the second baseman is the cutoff, and is positioned in line with second base and the outfielder who gets the ball, about 15 to 20 feet from the base (or farther given the outfielder's throwing

3–8. **CUTOFF PLAY WITH BASES EMPTY**

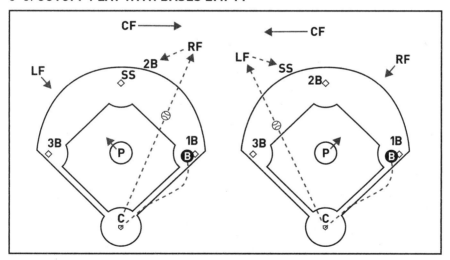

A: Ball hit to right side. Second baseman stands 15 feet off bag if shallow hit, and moves out toward outfielder if further relay is needed. Shortstop covers bag.

B: Ball hit to left side. Shortstop stands 15 feet off if shallow hit, and moves out toward outfielder if further relay is needed. Second baseman covers bag.

3-9. CUTOFF PLAY WITH LEAD RUNNER ON FIRST

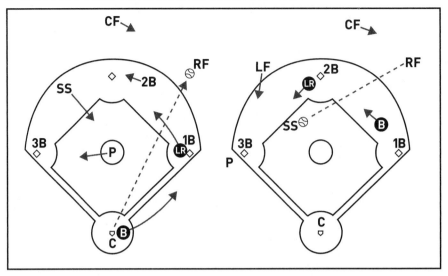

A: Start of play. Ball hit to right field. Lead runner (LR) on first.

B: Proper position. Right fielder throws toward third base in front of lead runner. Shortstop is cutoff to hold batter at first. Pitcher backs up third base by 15 feet.

ability). The shortstop covers second base. These two players reverse position on a hit to the left side, in which case the shortstop is the cutoff. (See figure 3-8 on page 55.)

Runner on first base only. We know a runner on first will get to second base easily on a base hit, so we want to hold him at second. Therefore, the outfielder will throw toward third, and in this situation the shortstop is the cutoff. (See figure 3-9.) The second baseman plays close to the bag to try to hold the runner on second base. As the ball comes in from the outfield, the shortstop must decide whether to let the ball go through to the third baseman or to cut it off. If the lead runner has stopped at second, the shortstop should cut it off. If the runner has tried to reach third, the third baseman must tell the shortstop whether to cut it off by shouting, "Cut it!" (if there is no play or if the throw is off line) or to let it go through by shouting, "Through." If the ball is cut off, the shortstop then looks to the batter to see if there is a play against him going to second base. The pitcher always backs up third base on a play to third.

Runner on first and second, or second base only. In these situations, the lead runner is on second. This runner is in scoring position and must be openly recognized as such. Yell out, "Lead runner on second." The goal is to stop the runner from going home on a single, so the outfielder throws ahead of the lead runner; he throws home. The chatter should reach a fever pitch here since a runner is in scoring position. The whole team needs to understand that this runner is a threat. For this play, the cutoff is the pitcher. (See figure 3-10.)

The pitcher is the closest player to home. If there is a play at the plate, the pitcher is my cutoff choice. He first looks at the ball to see if it was thrown straight. If it was not, he will probably have to cut it off, since they will not get the runner at the plate anyway, and he needs to make sure the other runners don't advance.

Now, I know I'll catch some flak here, because in big league play the pitcher always backs up home when there is a possible play at the plate, and depending on which side the ball is hit to, the third baseman or the first baseman is the cutoff. Actually, at advanced levels of play on Major League-sized fields and even on "50-70" fields, there are different scenarios for cutoff and backing up, depending on the number of runners and the depth of the hit. At high school and college levels, the kids play every day, and have time to practice these plays. At young ages, you need to keep it a bit simpler. Just getting it in to second base may be the

3-10. **CUTOFF PLAY WITH LEAD RUNNER ON SECOND**

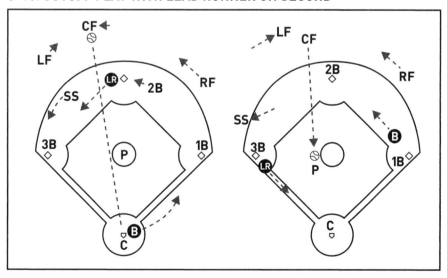

A: Start of play. Ball hit to center field. Lead runner (LR) on second base.

B: Proper position. Center fielder throws ahead of lead runner threatening toward home. Pitcher is cutoff to hold batter at first.

best you can accomplish. I believe coaches need to get what they can, and then push a bit further. If you understand the concept, you can tell you kids what to do in given situations.

After the first edition of this book came out, I got a call from a coach in Seattle who had an assistant coach who was arguing with him about my cutoff locations. The assistant had played college ball and felt that the big-league cutoff responsibilities should be taught. Well, my response was that the kids weren't playing on a big-league field. A Little League field is smaller, has a much closer backstop to the plate area, and involves a shorter throw from the outfield. Therefore, the cutoff game should be tailored to the field at hand, and to what the kids can do, how far they can throw, and what they can grasp. I like the pitcher in the middle on a play at the plate, and if he lets the ball through, he can, and should, still come in and help the catcher if it squirts by. When the kids move up to bigger fields, the pitcher goes behind the catcher with a lead runner on second, and the infield corners can do the cutoff. On most Little-League fields, the backstop does the job, and so the pitcher is more useful as a cutoff on a throw home.

If you teach the pitcher to back up home and want the first or third baseman to be cutoff on a play at the plate, that's fine. I taught that when my kids moved to 90-foot bases. I just found that my way worked better and was simpler for young players.

Read this section a few times. Once you have the concept in mind, you will automatically know what to do. The general concept that you must etch onto the fielders' minds is to throw toward the base in front of the lead runner. The coach must designate a fielder who should be ready to cut off that throw to keep the batter or another runner from advancing. The cutoff may vary a bit depending on how well outfielders can throw, but most kids can get the ball into the infield on a base hit.

Using a cutoff is not a matter of memorizing what to do. It's a principle that is simply to stop the lead runner by throwing ahead of him and to give fielders a shot at other runners by hitting the cutoff. The team chatters to each other, with the coach's help, about who the lead runner is, who the cutoff is, and what base the outfielder must throw to. This chatter goes on incessantly before each pitch.

It's best for kids to learn the concepts behind what they need to do. Then they can figure out what to do in a given play. I adjust things based on the abilities of fielders. Again, field chatter is the best way to get these ideas to sink in. Constantly remind players who the lead runners are.

That's what the cutoff is about. It's logical and really very simple when you think about it. The purpose of defense is to stop runs from being scored. The outfielders therefore try to get the ball in front of the lead runner. They direct the ball to the next

3-11. CUTOFF PLAY ON A DEEP HIT TO THE FENCE

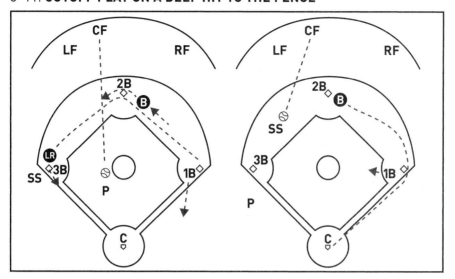

A: A runner on first (LR) at the start of the play will likely reach third base easily, so the outfielder or relay (2B if needed) should throw toward home, to the cutoff (pitcher). Shortstop backs up third base.

B: With no one on, the batter (B) will likely reach second base, so throw toward third base, to the cutoff (shortstop). Pitcher backs up third base.

base to which the lead runner would go. If there is a chance to get that runner out, the ball is allowed to go through. If there is no play, the cutoff fielder catches the ball to see if he can make a play on the other runners to stop then from advancing. The more you go over the concept, the simpler it will become to your team.

Of course, when the ball goes past the outfielder, to the fence, the concept is the same, but the second baseman or shortstop has to go out farther to get the relay. Children can't throw the ball to the plate from 200 feet away. So the shortstop or second baseman, depending on which side of the field the ball is on, goes out to get the relay and then turns to make the play. The other infielders can help by yelling to the cutoff and pointing where to throw the ball. On a ball hit to the fence, runners on second or third base will score. The defense's only hope is to stop the runner on first (if there is one) from going home, or to catch the batter going to second base (if he is slow) or to third base. (See figure 3-11.) Since these are the only plays possible, outfielders should focus on throwing to third if no one is on base, or to second base to catch a slow runner, or home if a runner is on first base. Ignore the other runners, since they will score.

The cutoff takes the throw from the deep outfielder and wheels to throw to home or to third depending on the situation.

RUNDOWNS

Often a runner is caught between two bases. This situation calls for a *rundown*. It's a simple play, but one that is often fouled up. Its elements are as follows.

TOP SIX KEYS TO RUNDOWNS

1. Get the runner to fully commit himself. Whoever has the ball, usually an infielder, must understand that the runner wants to see where the ball will be thrown so that he can run in the opposite direction. Therefore, the fielder should charge at the runner and get him to commit to a direction first.

2. Get the ball quickly to the next base. You always want to force the runner back to the prior base and attempt the putout there. That way, if the putout fails, at least the runner will not have advanced. This is particularly important, for obvious reasons, when the rundown is between third base and home plate.

3. Feigning the throw. The fielder with the ball should hold it high, feigning a throw while running hard on the inside of the basepath. The feign will confuse the runner, who is trying to anticipate the throw. The position on the inside of the basepath allows for an open throw to the baseman, without hitting the runner with the ball. A good faked throw may get the runner to stop or to change direction, allowing the fielder to tag him. A well-executed rundown should require only one throw to retire the runner. (See figure 3-12 on page 61.)

4. The rest is "feel"—if the fielder can make the tag, he does so. Otherwise, the player with the ball throws to the base in time for the baseman to make the tag. He should make a snap throw, mainly using the wrist with little arm movement.

5. Stay off the base. The fielder covering the base toward which the runner is heading should be off the base by at least several feet toward the runner on the inside of the basepath. Then, if the throw is a bit late, he still has time to make a tag. How many times has a runner slid under a late throw to a baseman standing on the bag? If you see a rundown in the pros, the receiving fielder is usually off the bag and calls for the throw when the runner is close. Note: All fielders should play slightly to the inside basepath to avoid hitting the runner with the ball.

3-12. RUNDOWN

Chase runner to prior base, hold ball high, inside the runner.

6. Backing each other up. Any available fielders who are not guarding other runners should back up the fielders involved in the rundown. They are often needed if the ball is overthrown.

Rundown Home Drill. Have a runner stand midway between third base and home. The coach should throw the ball to the catcher to initiate the drill. The runner tries to avoid getting tagged. The third baseman takes two steps in, the shortstop gets just behind third, and the pitcher backs up the catcher at home. Fielders run the player back toward third base, and try to get him out.

04 RUNNING AND SLIDING

One great thing about baseball is that the part that is the most fun—hitting—is also the easiest to teach, and improvement can be rapid. Running ability, and speed in particular, is like fielding: If you don't have it naturally, you can improve only with a great deal of practice. I repeat that the adage that you can't make a kid into a fielder or a pitcher or a runner is not true. But it does take longer, and the key is just doing a lot of it.

Usually, kids who are slower play third base, first base, or catcher, since they don't need as much speed or range at those positions. They need quickness and good reflexes; they just don't need speed.

However, speed in the outfield and quickness in the infield do win games. Speed on the basepath will score more runs, so a fast kid will get more playing time.

For young kids, you can increase speed by running wind sprints. A good workout is a half-dozen 30-yard dashes. Make sure to have players warm up first! Sprints give additional strength to get up to speed more quickly; acceleration comes from leg strength. Proper running form is on the balls of the toes, body as low as possible, head and shoulders forward, arms churning up and down. (See figure 4-1 on page 63). Running form is often not taught in baseball, but it is an essential skill. Get your players on their toes, with their bodies low. Conduct races to make learning how to run more fun.

Running up stairs or hills is good for quickness. There is a difference between quickness and speed. Quickness is mobility over a short distance. A child can improve quickness more easily than speed. (See the speed and agility drills in chapter seven.) As noted earlier, defensive players always need to be on their toes, weight forward, body hunched forward and down to lower the center of gravity. Keeping the weight on the toes also allows the infielder to move, spring, and hop as needed to field the ball and to quickly switch to a throwing stance.

EIGHT BASICS FOR RUNNING BASES

Base runners have to do the same thing—weight down and forward, on the balls of the feet, ready to spring. A player running to a base, especially first base, should always run as fast as possible. Many times a player is out at first base because he turned to see where the ball was or slowed just before he got to the base. The runner should simply put his head down and run like there's no tomorrow. Here are eight other essentials to base running:

1. Explode from the box. When the runner runs to first base on an infield hit, the process begins in the batter's box. Many hits are lost when a kid gets a slow start out of the box. Once contact is made, the batter must not worry about where the ball is; his first instinct must be to run, to explode from the box. A righty batter should push off with the left foot, take a small step with the right foot, lower the body, and start pumping the arms.

2. Sprint to each base. Quite often a player will try to follow the flight of the ball, instead of running as quickly as possible. It's important to not lose time and precious steps by being a spectator. Tell your players to focus on the next base and run hard. When you talk about running, talk about the need to lower the center of gravity, stay on the toes, look for chances to run, and run hard when you go. Make a list of the basics and yell them out every so often. Repetition works.

4-1. **RUNNING**

Body low, arms churning, head and shoulders forward.

63

3. Run through the bag at first base. Runners should run hard and *through* the bag at first base. They should not hop onto it, but run through it. A player may overrun first base by as much as needed to slow down. Some people erroneously think that a runner can't turn toward second base. There is no rule on which way to turn, and the runner can safely return to first as long as he did not make a move that appears to be an attempt to go to second base. It's a good practice, however, to turn away from the field.

4. Hook pattern. If the ball was hit to the outfield, the runner should run a hook pattern toward the base. (See figure 4-2 A.) This means that the runner makes an arc, about 6 to 8 feet into foul territory on a Little League-size field. He should start to make the arc about halfway or more to first base. The arc helps to set the runner on a more direct course to second base if he chooses to go.

Go/Fence Drill. Line players up at home plate and have them run to first base at full speed. The coach yells, "Go, Go!" to indicate the runner should make the hook pattern turn (see figure 4–2) and go to second, or "Fence, fence!" in which case the player runs through the bag and turns toward the fence to the right. I've seen this drill called "Go/Dugout," but I like the word *fence* better since it's one syllable and can be said faster.

5. Inside foot to inside corner. When a runner is going to advance to the next base, he should plant his left foot on the inside corner of the bag and lean into the turn. This

4-2. RUNNING BASES

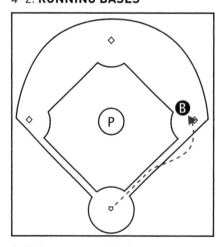

A: Hook pattern rounding first base.

B: Plant foot on inside corner and lean in.

can save much time, and a step or two. (See figure 4-2 B.) The base can be touched with either foot, however, so players don't get jumbled up, but the left foot is preferable.

6. Expect to take another base. Especially when running to first base with second base open (no runner on second), and when the throw from the outfield may head to third base or home with an opportunity to advance, a runner needs to go all out. He runs through first base looking for an opportunity to go farther, making the turn if it's safe and advancing a bit toward second base.

Once the runner gets near any base, he must look for the ball and decide whether to advance. Runners should always know where the ball is and watch or anticipate where and how hard it will be thrown. A runner must look at the base coach to see if he is motioning to stay or advance, but often the runner needs to rely on his own judgment. I like my runners to lull the outfielders by pretending they are going to stop (if the outfielder is preparing to throw), but get as much ground as they can. Then if the throw is not good, or if it's not to the base in front of them, they can sprint to that base. A runner who hits the ball to the outfield should go about a quarter to a third of the way to second base, and then see if the throw is other than to the bag in front of him—if not, he goes. Many kids can cover the remaining distance before someone can catch the throw and relay it to the second baseman. After some practice, a child will know what he is able to do. The point is that a runner is *always looking to advance safely*.

7. Halfway on a fly ball. Upon a fly ball to the outfield, a runner on first base should advance about halfway to second to see if the ball will be caught. If caught, he must return to tag up. If the ball is not caught, he has already covered half the distance and may now be able to go to third base. Actually, on a fly to left, he can go more than halfway, and on a fly to right he should go less than halfway ... but start with half and refine from there.

8. Bounce and look. If an unforced runner is on second or third with less than two outs, the runner should bounce off the bag a few steps on a grounder to get enough of a lead to advance upon a throw to first. If the ball is hit to a nearby fielder, obviously the bounce is minimal, but if it's to a fielder farther away, then a good bounce is possible. As the ball is released, the runner then sprints to the next base.

In chapter three we reviewed the concept of throwing in front of the lead runner. Well, the offensive side is that the lead runner should look for chances to advance an extra base, especially if the ball isn't thrown ahead of him. Runners should always make things happen, taking a wide turn at a base—not so wide that they can't get back safely—but wide enough to draw a throw. If the throw is bad, they go. Some

04

boys are so fast that they automatically go when the ball is thrown behind them because they know they will beat the next relay.

BASE COACHING

For me, one of the joys of managing a youth team is coaching third base. Most rules allow at least one coach on the baselines, so take advantage of it. Out on the field is where the action is, and good coaches should be close to it. Third base is my favorite spot. Coaches are essential at third base since the decision to send a runner home is such an important one.

As noted earlier, the main strategy at youth ages, particularly for kids under twelve years old, is to keep the kids running. Take risks—they usually pay off. It takes a good throw, a good catch, *and* a good tag to get a runner out, and getting all three at once is more the exception than the rule at young ages.

When a runner approaches third, he must do one of four things: (1) run to the bag and stay on it, (2) slide into it, (3) take a turn for a few steps toward home to draw a throw or to be ready to sprint home if an opportunity arises, or (4) run through the base at full speed and sprint home. The sign for the first option is both hands up overhead, signaling, "Stop! No need to slide. The ball is not close, but stay on the bag."

The signal to slide is both hands down, palms down. When it's real close, I lie right down on the ground to signal that a low, low slide is needed. I point to the side of the bag that the runner should slide toward, usually the inside. The runner should then look not at the ball, but at the location of the fielder's glove to see how to avoid the tag.

The signal to take a wide turn is to raise the left hand, open palm in a halting signal, and then point with the right hand to the spot on the ground that the player should run to. Pick a spot 5 to 10 feet past the base. The runner and the coach then look toward the ball to see if any possibility arises to run home. The runner must stay close enough to the bag to dart back if the defense makes a play on him.

If the coach wants to send the runner home, he windmills his extended left arm clockwise. You can even run a few steps with the runner to encourage him to dig hard and slide low at the plate.

With a runner on third and less than two outs, I repeatedly warn the player to stand on the bag if the ball is hit to the outfield. This is so he can tag up and score. I tell him not to look at the ball, but just to listen for my "go" signal.

The first-base coach must encourage the runner to dig hard and beat the throw. He must also remind the runner on first of how many outs there are; whether second base is open; to advance halfway to second on a fly ball; and to look for the third-base coach's signal.

SIGNALS

Not all coaches use signals for the batter and runners on the pitch. This is because there are few bunts and most steals are on passed balls. However, signals are part of baseball. They are useful at all levels, and kids need to learn the concepts.

Signals are a series of hand movements touching the coach's body, such as touching the bill of the hat, the mouth, the chest, a shoulder, the elbow, or clapping hands. A typical set might be: touch the cap bill = a steal; touch the chin = take a pitch (don't swing); touch the chest = bunt; touch a shoulder = hit and run. Other signals can be used to call for a fake bunt, a hit to the right side of the infield, a swing at the first pitch, or a sacrifice. Once you have a set of signals, don't change them. Let the kids get used to them.

The way to stop the other teams from stealing your signs is to have a *key* signal that means that the *next signal* is the one to follow. For example, a key signal might be touching the top of the head. So, using the above signs, a steal would be signaled by (1) a series of dummy signs, (2) touching the top of the head, (3) touching the bill of the cap, and then (4) finishing with a few other dummy signs. Once the batter or runners (all of whom must be watching your signs) see you touch the top of your head, they know the next sign is the real one.

Simon Signs Drill. Call the team together and run through the various signs, using a key signal. Let them call out the signal you are sending.

STEALING BASES

After walks, and there seems to be a million of them, stealing bases is the worst part of youth baseball. Under twelve years old, the distance between bases is very short, and the rule against taking a lead makes it very, very hard to steal except on a ball missed by the catcher (passed ball). However, there are so many passed balls and wild pitches that runners pretty much advance at will. Occasionally, you get a decent catcher who will limit stealing, but stealing on passed balls dominates the game. I don't like it, but that's the way it is.

So keep your players running. Some leagues prohibit stealing, or at least stealing home. I agree with that because makes kids hit the ball. But until they change the rules, keep the kids running because opposing teams surely will.

There are times to steal and times to hold. The best time to steal is with two outs and the only runner on first. A steal may get him into scoring position, which is particularly helpful in a close game. The worst time to steal is when the other team has a large lead. Outs are valuable when you are behind, and it's not good to waste one on a marginal steal. When you have a big lead, it's poor form to rub it in, but I've learned that no lead is large enough to guarantee victory in youth baseball. I've held kids up with a ten-run lead and gone on to lose by one run. You can be darned if you do and darned if you don't!

As noted earlier, some leagues have moved to larger fields for twelve year olds and for younger All-Star teams. Bases are 10 feet farther apart, set at 70 feet, and kids are allowed to take a lead. This adds more offense, more running, and more excitement to the game, but it also seems to put an emphasis on stealing, since not all catchers are alike, and many get run on routinely. Overall, I like the new rule and expect the kids will adjust to it.

STEAL ON THE PITCHER

With the longer basepaths discussed above, stealing is authorized at any time, and runners may take a lead. Pitchers must hold runners close to the base by occasionally throwing to the base, but may not *balk*, interrupt any movement associated with delivering the ball to home plate. A balk may occur when a pitcher tries to catch a runner off base with a pick-off throw after he has started his delivery to the batter. Runners look for the pitcher's first move, usually the pitcher's hip, knee, or foot making a move toward home plate, or if he lifts his hands to begin the stride. At that moment, a runner intending to steal begins to run. The pitcher cannot stop the pitch to try to throw out the runner, and must deliver the ball home.

DELAYED STEALS

A fun play is to steal home. If the catcher is sloppy about throws to the pitcher, have your base coaches keep the kids ready to run, especially runners at second or third. Tell the runner on third to advance about 5 to 6 feet on the pitch (as the ball passes the batter), then to stand quietly, trying not to draw the catcher's attention. As the catcher prepares to throw to the pitcher, grab a few more feet, and then as the catcher starts to throw, run home. If the pitcher stays on the mound, it can be done easily. Often, a pitcher will walk off the mound toward the catcher to get the throw, and then it will not work well. If the catcher has a lazy arm, keep 'em running all day!

SLIDING

Sliding is an important part of base running. Very often, the success or failure of a steal depends on how good the slide is. Coaches often don't teach sliding since it can scrape a runner's side or leg. It may be that the ground is too hard, or the coach doesn't feel he has time. But there are basics to sliding, and it can and should be safely practiced.

The technique to sliding is demonstrated in figure 4-3. In a slide, the runner lifts his arms up and then sits down. The right leg is bent and tucked in under the left, and the slide is pretty much flat on the right side of the butt. The key to sliding is to keep every part of the body low to the ground. The best slide is one where the player is virtually lying down on his back at the time of contact. Players should avoid breaking the fall with their hands; it's very easy to sprain a wrist. Besides, the backside gives enough cushion. Keep the hands up, off the ground, but not so high that they can be tagged.

The player should slide away from the ball. On a throw from the outfield, he should slide inside the base. Here, he tucks in the left leg and reaches with the right. For a play at the plate, he slides to the umpire side of home plate, away from the throw. This is called a *hook slide*. When practicing, stand by the bag with the glove low and have the players think about getting under the tag.

Some aggressive players slide head first, diving at the base. It does get you there more quickly, but it's very dangerous. I've seen sprained wrists and bloody noses, even a broken back. Of course, at twelve years old or younger, kids don't need to dive. If it happens, caution the player against it. It's not worth the risk.

Slide Drill. Have kids practice sliding by using a large piece of cardboard, like a refrigerator box. Lay it on the ground. The kids should take off their shoes and run and slide on the cardboard. It works and they love it. Thick grass also works for practice.

4-3. SLIDING

Throw the left foot toward the base, bend the right leg for a cushion, hands off the ground. (This picture shows the opposite, which is sometimes necessary, as explained above.) Slide low, and avoid the tag.

05 BASEBALL POSITIONS

At young ages, beginner and intermediate, kids should play various, if not all, positions. They certainly should practice at different positions. Early in the season, I have every boy on the team pitch during practice. During defensive drills, they play every position. It's good for them, and it helps me to see their skills and who is best for the more important positions up the middle—shortstop, second base, and center field. The earlier chapters of this book identified the basics that apply to each position, and you should try to spend some time on each area. Emphasize hitting, but work also on fielding, throwing, and running.

This chapter covers each individual position. It gives you an understanding of defensive concepts from the perspective of each position. This will add to your overview of the game and will help you decide which position a kid should play. If you are a parent, you can advise your child on which position he is best suited for, but be aware that a coach may see things differently.

CATCHER

No one can pick up a team like a catcher! Catchers face their teams most of the time and are in the best position to encourage fellow players and keep them on their toes. They see the full action and can shout out where the ball needs to go. A catcher should be a leader and an aggressive kid.

It takes a special kind of kid to hang in at this position. It's tough to get kids interested in being catcher and even tougher to find a good one. If you want to guarantee that your child plays a lot in each game, tell him to be a catcher. He'll play all he wants at that position.

Catchers are usually very tough-minded kids. They have to be able to take some pain. The ball often strains the thumb of the catching hand. Catchers get bruised by the ball and run over by runners. It's dirty and hot underneath all of the equipment. They must move up and down on every pitch and must be into the game more than anyone on the field.

As noted earlier, catching is also good for a big kid (or any size kid) who doesn't have the speed needed for other defensive positions. There is a defensive position for everybody—and if a player can hit well, you must find a position he can play.

TOP TEN FUNDAMENTALS OF CATCHING

1. Stance. A catcher must get used to crouching on the toes of both feet. If he is a righty, the right foot is back a bit. Weight should be forward on the balls of the feet, heels lightly touching the ground. Putting one knee down on the ground is no good. It reduces mobility and agility, and it increases the risk of injury. The upper leg is parallel to the ground, and the waist is bent forward. Catchers are "ready:" Weight is balanced on the toes, and they are able to move quickly and freely from side to side to retrieve a bad pitch, or to throw upon a steal attempt. (See figure 5-1 on page 72.) Often, kids will tire and "sit" on their haunches or rest some weight on one knee. Doing this inhibits mobility, so encourage them to crouch when the pitch is delivered.

Young catchers often get too far back behind the plate. Obviously, they worry about getting hit with the bat. They don't realize that the batter is stepping forward, his body moving toward the pitcher, and that the bat will not hit them. They must be closer to the batters because that is where the strike zone is. If they move back too far, the pitcher has to throw higher to reach the glove. Also, as the catcher moves back from the batter, the strike zone shrinks from the umpire's perspective. Tell the catcher to set up with his glove just an inch or two behind the batter's hands or elbow, whichever is the batter's backmost point.

2. Let the ball come to the glove. If the catcher reaches out for the ball, there is a chance that the bat will nick the glove. This doesn't happen often, but when it does, the batter gets a free trip to first base. Pitches above the waist should be caught with the fingers up; low pitches should be caught with the fingers down. The glove hand is soft, receiving the ball (not stabbing at it) and gently pulling it back to the chest.

3. Catch the ball one-handed. The catcher's free hand should be behind his back or behind his leg. Some kids put it behind the glove, and that is certainly less dangerous than keeping it exposed. I like it behind the back; I've seen too many bad bruises otherwise. The free hand can get hit by the bat or by a foul tip. Keeping the hand

05

71

5-1. **CATCHING POSITION**

Great stance. Low crouch. Weight forward on balls of toes. Right foot back a bit. Upper leg parallel to ground. Good target. Free hand behind back.

5-2. **BLOCKING LOW PITCHES**

Low pitch over the plate. Drop knees and collapse body to block the ball.

behind some part of the body, fist clenched, protects it. The ball should always be caught in the pocket of the glove.

4. Control the pitcher's tempo. One of the key jobs of a catcher is to keep the pitcher's emotions in check. The catcher should constantly talk to the pitcher, trying to keep him focused on the batter and pitching at an even tempo, not too fast or slow. He must remind him to keep pitching "over the top," instead of relaxing into a sidearm motion, and to follow through when he starts getting tired. He should remind the pitcher to drive hard off the back foot. The catcher should keep reminding the pitcher of the location of the catcher's glove—"Hit the glove, here it is, pop the glove, baby." The catcher should pound the glove with his free hand, move the glove around a bit, open and close it, shake it—anything to get the pitcher to focus on the glove. The catcher should slow the pitcher's rate of pitching if he starts to rush, particularly if the ball starts regularly coming in high. The catcher should stand up, walk around, and slow the pitcher down, so he takes time to concentrate.

5. Stop the pitch in the dirt. Another important thing a catcher does is to stop (or trap) low pitches. A pitch in the dirt is tough to catch, so the priority is to block it. Tell your catcher to drop to the knees, dropping the glove low, fingers down, and to concentrate on blocking the ball. If it goes into the glove, fine. It will at least be nearby. If the pitch is low and to one side, drop the closest knee in front of the ball and try to keep the body facing forward to block if the ball comes up. (See figure 5-2 on page 72.) If your child is a catcher, ask the coach to borrow the gear or to keep it at home for the season. With this equipment, your kid can practice catching low pitches at home. Put some extra padding on the exposed areas such as the thighs and arms. Throw low pitches from about half the distance to the mound. Use a hard, rubber-coated ball at first. Make sure the chin stays down to cover the neck and throat, and make double sure the throat guard is attached to the mask.

6. Shoot the runner. Another very important job of a catcher is to throw out players who are stealing. The throw to second base is the main throw a catcher will make. The idea is to get the ball to the fielder's glove about a foot off the ground and a foot right of the base. It's okay to throw the ball on one hop, so it comes in low, rather than to throw high. The catcher should come up from the crouch, driving off the back right foot (for a righty), quickly transition the ball from the glove to the hand, and fire at the spot where the fielder's glove should be. Practice this move.

A good practice drill is to get the catcher in a crouch position and to throw the ball behind him to the backstop. The catcher turns and runs to the ball, taking off his mask as he runs and throwing it to the side; then he picks up the ball and turns again, firing the ball to second base. Practice this several times each session. After a while, he will know how much time it has taken to get to the ball and whether he will have a play. Have a base runner run from first to second to learn timing. If the runner is stealing third, the catcher must be sure he has a play before throwing the ball. A bad throw will cost a run. Many coaches practice the throw to second, but the throw to third is more important.

In Little League, a kid usually steals only on a passed ball or wild pitch. However, when the runners may take a lead, they may steal at will. The catcher must assess the runner's speed and the size of the lead taken, and ready himself for a steal attempt. Such a steal situation requires the catcher to be in a proper crouch, legs spread, up on his haunches as much as possible. Teammates will usually yell "steal" when a steal is attempted; the catcher should not lose focus on the ball, so he should listen for his teammates' signal. The key to throwing out a runner is the quickness with which the catcher is able to get the ball out of his glove and into throwing position. A quick transition of ball from glove to hand is essential, as is a quick move into throwing position. As soon as the ball hits the glove, the catcher reaches for it and drives off his right foot (for righties), stepping toward the target. Practice this move repeatedly.

73

5-3. **PLAY AT THE PLATE**

A: Awaiting the throw. Place left foot just inside the plate as the ball approaches (not too early!).

B: Proper tag position. In front of plate, left leg blocking plate, two hands on the ball. Bring the right knee and glove down quickly, and tag low. Brace the body for a collision.

7. Block the plate and tag with two hands. A most important job of the catcher is to be able to get the runner out at the plate. Often, the ball is thrown hurriedly, and is off line or in the dirt. Have catchers practice getting throws in the dirt, so they learn how to stop a bad throw. The catcher stands right in front of home plate, and if the ball arrives in time for a tag, he should turn and block the plate with the left foot, catch the ball with two hands (it must be two hands, since a collision is coming!), and bring the glove downward quickly to tag the runner's feet. Usually, in youth ball, the runner must slide or he is out, so the tag will always be low. Contrary to the image above, the catcher should have his mask off; in fact, the mask should come off automatically every time the ball is hit. It's a lot easier to catch a ball at the plate if you can see it, so catchers must get the mask off and throw it into foul territory. (See figures 5-3 A,B.)

8. Look for the foul pop-up. A catcher should also practice catching pop fouls. Usually, youth ball backstops have an overhang to prevent most foul tips from going far, but there may still be some that are playable. A good drill is for a coach to stand at the plate and just throw the ball straight up. It's difficult, but the idea is to look up quickly. Catchers also need to get used to "picking the ball up" as it comes off the bat.

9. Snatch and lob. When a runner steals home on a passed ball (and this will happen seemingly a million times), the catcher really needs to move quickly. He runs to the ball and snatches it, lobbing it to the pitcher who is covering home plate. It must be in

5-4. SNATCH AND LOB

Catcher jumps to the ball, snatches it, and lobs to a point 12 inches above the plate in one motion.

all one motion; if it's done quickly, the runner can be tagged. The lob should be a foot off the ground, just to the runner's side of the bag, so that the pitcher can catch it and drop the tag. Practice this move. It will save games. (See figure 5-4.)

10. Watch the bunt. We see more bunts now in youth ball than years ago, and that's good for baseball. There are also many swings that just tap the ball down, resulting in a bunt-type roll. A catcher should always try to field any ball he can get to, since it's hard for the pitcher to come in and throw to the direction opposite his momentum. Tell your catcher to make sure he has an open angle to the first baseman so he doesn't hit the runner in the back. The key is to approach the ball from the left side and, if necessary, take a step toward the pitcher before throwing.

FIRST BASE

I played a lot at first base over the years. I was tall, had a decent glove, was not very fast, and I could hit. These are good ingredients for a first baseman. Add in a lefty, and it's perfect. A lefty doesn't have to rotate once he gets to the bag to get the glove hand out to the throw like a righty does. A lefty also has an easier throw to second base, and the angle makes it less likely that a lefty throw will hit a runner.

In youth play, first base is very important. Your whole infield is as good as your first baseman. The shortstop can make a great play and a good throw, but if the first baseman drops the ball or comes off the bag too early, that fielding effort was worthless.

75

It happens countless times in youth league play. If your child can catch hard throws and is able to adjust to get a ball that is thrown a bit off line, he can play first base.

KEYS TO PLAYING FIRST BASE

1. Get to the bag. A first baseman has one critical job—to be in position and catch the ball when it's thrown to him. When a grounder is hit to another infielder, the first baseman must *spring* to the bag quickly. He doesn't have to watch the ball; he has to look at the bag and get to it quickly. He must be ready for the throw, and set up in proper position to present a good target for the throw.

2. Have proper stance. When he gets to the bag, he puts the ball of his back foot's toe, the foot opposite his glove hand, on the inside edge of the bag and faces the fielder with the glove chest-high. He doesn't stretch yet, not until he sees where the ball is going, since the throw could be errant, requiring him to adjust. Then he steps toward the ball, stretching only as far as he needs to, to catch the ball for the out. (See figure 5-5.) Note that his foot always touches the bag. If the play is not close and the ball is well thrown, the first baseman may need only a small step to catch the ball in a comfortable posture. However, in youth play, the distance to first base is not great, so many plays are close, and a stretch may be needed to ensure the ball hits the glove before the runner touches the bag. If the ball is thrown a bit off line, a long stretch may be needed to catch the ball. I've seen first basemen who can stretch into a full split, which is very effective and really looks sharp if a player can do it.

3. Get to the ball. If the throw is bad, the first baseman's primary job is to stop the ball from going through to the fence. If he can do that while touching the bag, swell. But

5-5. FIRST BASEMAN'S STRETCH

Determine the path of the ball before stretching. Don't overstretch. Step toward the throw.

if he has to leave the bag to catch the ball, he *must* do so. Otherwise, the batter will go to second base and be in a scoring position. If the throw is wide to the left, the first baseman's first thought should be to catch the ball and then tag the runner, sweeping the glove to the left. In Little League, many throws are high. The first baseman should practice the timing needed to jump for the ball. If it's clearly out of reach, he should not waste time looking at it, but turn and run to where it will go—this may stop the runner from advancing to second. He should make sure he doesn't collide with the runner, though. The runner will be going full speed, and it can hurt.

4. Play the hop. The toughest ball for a first baseman to catch, as with the catcher, is one in the dirt, particularly if he is stretched out. Even a very good fielder is handicapped by the fact that his foot must stay on the bag, which limits agility and reflexes. I used to have my first basemen practice catching balls thrown in the dirt while wearing full catcher's gear and a "cup." This eliminates the fear of a bad hop into the face, chest, or neck. Practicing with a rubber-coated ball also helps. Players must learn to keep the head down, eyes on the ball. Tell them to concentrate on the bounce, and "see" the whole ball. First basemen have the biggest glove on the field, which helps to make tough catches.

5. Go for all grounders. When a grounder is hit to the first baseman, or between him and the second baseman, he must always try to get it. I've seen many grounders go between the two fielders because the first baseman hesitates, feeling he should cover the bag. On such a grounder, the pitcher has to cover first base. The first baseman should *always* try to make the field play. It's good to practice the lob from the first baseman to the pitcher. It's a tough play for the pitcher, since he is on the run and must look for the bag, then find the ball. The idea is to get the ball to him as soon as possible. The first baseman should hold the ball so the pitcher can see it and lob it at his glove. He keeps the arm fairly straight and leads the pitcher as much as is needed not to slow his pace.

6. Know the area. The first baseman also has to be ready to catch foul pops to the left side. The dugouts and fences are quite close, and he needs to practice knowing where they are. Have him count the steps on a dead run to the fence during practice or pre-game warm-ups. He should look at the foul line and the fair ground near to see how it slopes and what will happen to a bunt or a slow roller along the line. He should look for small rocks in the infield and toss them out of the way.

7. Know where the runners are. It's important to know who is on base and whether they will attempt to advance on the throw to first base. A nerve-wracking situation for the first baseman arises when a runner is on third. I remember a play I was involved in when the shortstop got a grounder, looked at the runner on third to hold him there, and then threw to me. It was the tying run of the game, and just as the shortstop started to throw to me, the runner on third broke for home, and he was fast. Out of the corner of my eye, I saw him running, and I sensed that he might beat my throw home. So I came off the bag, giving up a sure out, and threw home. It was a smart play, my coach told me. The runner would surely have beaten the throw otherwise—it was just too bad I threw the ball over the catcher's head!

8. Be ready to cut off or back up. Once the batter goes to second base, the first baseman is free to do whatever is needed. It's likely the ball was hit to the fence or at least in the outfield gaps, so the first baseman can run toward the center of the infield and get in line to back up any relays or to act as a cutoff. As noted in chapter three, I like the pitcher to be the cutoff on most plays to the plate, since he is not needed behind the catcher in youth level play. However, on shots to the fence, the pitcher usually backs up third base, since the batter will get to second base and threaten third base. The first baseman can run in to be the cutoff for any play at the plate. If the ball will be thrown to second base, he must stay and back up the throw.

9. Hold the runner. When playing on the larger fields, the first baseman must stand near first base to *hold a runner*, that is, prevent the runner from taking too great a lead. The pitcher should throw once or twice to first base to threaten the runner a bit. Then, as the pitcher begins to throw to the batter, the first baseman should hop quickly to the right, to get into a better position to field a grounder hit to his side of the field. Sometimes, a first baseman will play behind the runner and fake a step toward the bag to try and make the runner lean or come back to first base. At the very least, this fake step will slow the runner.

SECOND BASE

In Little League, particularly under age eleven, the second baseman gets the most grounders, not the shortstop. The shortstop does not even get the second most; the pitcher gets the second most grounders. The shortstop gets the third most plays, and the first baseman is right there with him.

When I think of second basemen, I think of smart players with good gloves who are smaller and quick; they don't need a good arm. Remember, in baseball anybody of any size, speed, or strength can play if he is willing to practice and develop some simple skills. Take another look at the information in chapter three on fielding grounders.

KEYS TO PLAYING SECOND BASE

1. Set up in the proper location. Younger kids get the bat around slowly and drop the right side, so many balls go to the right side—right at the second baseman. Kids tend to play too close to the bag at second, but the proper positioning is about a third of the way to first base and 8 feet deeper than the baseline, toward the outfield.

2. Knock grounders down. A second baseman must be able to stop grounders. He doesn't need a good arm (infielders with good arms become shortstops or third basemen), but he does need to be quick. He's got to run down the grounders, and catch them or at least knock them down, so he can throw to first. Even if he just knocks grounders down, there is usually time to get the ball to first base since it is very close.

3. Have the proper stance. Chapter three discussed infielding generally: Fielders need to stay low, weight forward, knees bent, head down on the ball, eyes on the ball, glove low and raised forward to the ball in a scooping motion. An infielder has to be able to dance, on the toes. He springs to the ball and then hops into his throwing stance. If you look at the pros, they are always dancing around on the field.

4. Know ahead of time where to throw. The second baseman needs to be smart, too. There is plenty of action, and you want somebody who can think. Second basemen must know what to do with the ball when they get it. If nobody is on, they throw to first. With a runner on first, they throw to the shortstop for the force at second. If the second baseman is close to the bag, he takes a step and lobs the ball to the shortstop. If he is farther away from the bag, he pivots on his toes and throws sidearm.

With bases loaded and less than two outs, the coach has a choice of what to do with infield grounders. In a close game, I always say to throw home if you think you can stop the run; that's good baseball. Some coaches may not have faith in the catcher or the second baseman's arm, and will still want the sure out at second base. My approach is to teach my players the right way to play baseball, but different people have different views about what is right and about winning.

If there is a runner on third, and he is not forced to run home, the infielder should give him a look before throwing for the force at second or first. If the runner is going, then the infielder should throw home and get him out. Again, the purpose of defense is to stop runs, and that's the way the game should be taught.

5. Play around the bag. If a runner is on first and the ball is hit to the left side, the second baseman goes to the outfield side of second base to catch the throw from the shortstop or

05

third baseman, then steps on second, and pivots towards first, looking to see if he can get the ball to first for a double play. If the runner is sliding, the second baseman may need to hop over him to avoid being undercut. This hop-and-throw is one of the greatest plays in all of baseball. (See figure 5-6.) There are several ways to pivot on second base, depending on how close the runner is to the bag. Players can practice these by changing the timing and speed of the throw. If the batter is too close to first for a play, the second baseman should hold onto the ball—he doesn't want to throw it away. If there are runners on first and second, the same thing applies: Look for the force at second. Get the sure out. There are times you want to go to third, I suppose, but Little League players should go for the sure out.

6. Get all pop-ups. We'll discuss later how to communicate among fielders and who has priority to catch fly balls or pop-ups. However, the second baseman is the primary receiver on infield pop-ups for his side of the field, covering the space between the pitcher and first baseman. On any pop-up behind the pitcher or significantly behind the first baseman, the second baseman should get to the ball and call for it. The toughest catches are *Texas-leaguers*—shallow pops to the outfield. The second baseman must turn and run, timing a leap for the ball. Practice these since they occur often.

7. Cutoff. The second baseman is also the cutoff for outfield singles if the ball is hit to his side of the outfield and no one is on base. Read chapter three for the cutoff positions with runners on base. With anyone on base, the second baseman's responsibility on a single is to cover second base. Other players will cut off throws to third or home. But, if the ball is hit deep on the right side, past the outfielder to the fence, then the second baseman must go out to assist the relay. He is not technically a cutoff at that point; he is just going out to make a relay.

5–6. HOP AND THROW

A great baseball play at second base.

8. Steals. On steals, I usually have the second baseman back up the shortstop on the throw from the catcher. In the big leagues, whether the batter is righty or lefty and where the ball might be hit determines who backs up. Usually, on a righty batter, the second baseman covers for the steal, because the ball will more likely be hit to the shortstop, and he needs to stay put while the runner at first is breaking for second. But in Little League, the kids can't steal until the ball gets to the batter, so the situation is not the same. I think the shortstop can see the play better from his position. He can see the runner, so I let him make the tag. The second baseman backs up.

In games where runners are permitted to take a lead, the second baseman should also try to hold a runner on second base. Unlike first basemen, who often must stand near the bag to hold a runner, the middle infielders have too much ground to cover. So, they need to play a little *cat and mouse* with the runner. As the runner takes the lead and the pitcher glances back toward him just before the pitch, the second baseman will pretend or feint a move to the bag, trying to keep the runner off balance or otherwise shorten his lead. Every so often, the fielder should dash to the base to get a throw from the pitcher, perhaps in time to catch the runner off base and tag him out. These plays do not often work and often lead to an errant throw, allowing runners to advance. However, if practiced, they can work.

9. Bunts. The second baseman covers first base on bunts to the right side. The first baseman goes for the bunt, so someone needs to cover first base. The shortstop will cover second base.

SHORTSTOP

Shortstop is the most coveted defensive position after pitcher. This is true even though at beginner levels more balls are hit to second base. The best infielder will usually play at shortstop because the position requires all the defensive skills. By the time kids are playing "Major League" baseball (in Little League eleven and twelve year olds play in the "Major League"), the shortstop is the cornerstone of the defense. A shortstop is usually an excellent athlete. He can do it all, and at that position, you need it all. He must have a good glove, because batters "get around" on the ball and more balls are hit to the shortstop position. He also has to have a good arm because it's the longest infield throw, even longer than for the third baseman (who does not play as deep), and he often has to hurry the throw to beat the runner. A good throw from a shortstop is a pretty thing to see at Little League level, but often the throw is late or high.

05

Most teams put their best all-around player at shortstop (when he is not pitching). This doesn't mean your son can't play shortstop; it just means that he has to be the best if he wants to consistently play that position. And as I noted earlier, you don't have to be born with talent. Plenty of kids who are just average athletes work daily on their skills and become good enough to do the job. Any child can learn to do anything in baseball.

I'm not going to repeat everything I said in chapter three and summarized in the preceding section on second basemen. Much of the material about second basemen also pertains to shortstops.

KEYS TO PLAYING SHORTSTOP

1. Stance. The shortstop spreads his legs wide beyond the shoulders, bends his knees with his weight forward a bit, his right foot back some, and his toes pointing outward. His head is up, and his hands rest on his knees. When the pitcher strides, the short-stop moves a bit, raising his hands outward, keeping his eyes on the ball, and taking a slight step or hop forward.

2. Location. Since shortstops should play as deep "in the hole" as possible (that's about 12 feet back from the baseline toward the outfield, about one-third of the way toward third base), they face a long throw. The batter can reach first base at the eleven- to twelve-year-old level in just over three seconds, so there is little time to waste. The shortstop should circle around a ball to the right (for a better throwing position); on a ball to the left, he should use a crossover step.

3. Transition. More than for any other infielder, the shortstop has to make the transition from fielding to throwing as quickly as possible. This transition involves two moves. The first is to get the ball out of the glove into the throwing hand, and the second is to hop into a set throwing position. He plants the right foot squarely before throwing. (See chapter three on throwing positions.) When you practice with the shortstop, focus on making the transition quickly. Talk about the need for quickness and practice the transition repeatedly.

4. Double plays. With a runner on first, I like the shortstop to try to make the double play himself. If he is too far from second base, obviously he must throw the ball, but on a shot to his left, the shortstop should think about doing it himself. The throw to second always has the risk of being a problem. The second baseman needs time to change direction, and his throw is often off-balance. If the shortstop goes to second himself, these risks are eliminated. This is not true on the big league fields, but it's one of several things that are different for the smaller fields. Big league shortstops are too far from the bag to make double plays themselves.

5. Cutoff. The shortstop is the cutoff for base hits to the left side with no one on. I tell him to just stand 15 feet in front of second, with the second baseman backing him up on the bag. With a runner on first, the throw should go to third to stop the lead runner, and the shortstop is the cutoff for all three outfielders. He must line up between the ball and third base, about 15 to 25 feet from the bag, depending on which field the ball will come from (25 feet if from right field). He should know where the runner is, and if the batter heads for second base, the shortstop decides whether to cut the ball off and throw to second or to let the ball go through for a play at third. Obviously, if the throw is off line, there will be no play at third, so the shortstop must always cut the ball off.

On any ball hit past the outfielder on his side, the shortstop must go out far enough to get the relay throw, and he should know what he's going to do with the ball when he gets it—this is where the other infielders can help by telling the shortstop where to go. Generally, on an extra base hit, a runner on first will easily get to third, so the throw will be to home. If bases are empty, the batter will likely get to second, so the relay will go to third.

6. Pop-ups. The shortstop covers all shallow pop-ups on his side of the diamond and all pop-ups behind the third baseman. He plays deeper than the third baseman and can cover behind the third baseman more easily. Obviously, a fielder always has to call for the ball. Players should not rush to call too early, but the shortstop's call is law.

7. Calling for the ball. Many coaches teach that the first player who calls for a ball gets it. Some teach that the second player (or last player) to call for the ball gets it, but that player must call off the first player very loudly and repeatedly. Coaches do this for several reasons. First, the first one who calls often does so too soon, out of instinct. Second, the wind can change circumstances very quickly. Third, the second caller had more time to determine that his position is better. This doesn't mean that he is a better catcher; just that he is in a better position than the first player. In any event, if two players call for the ball, someone has to get it, and the rule should be firm either way.

I preferred to set general *rules of priority* on calling the ball. For instance, the center fielder has priority over anybody; any outfielder has priority over an infielder; a shortstop has priority over any infield ball; the second baseman has priority over other infielders on his side of the infield subject to the shortstop's priority; the pitcher has priority over the catcher; the catcher has priority over no one (because the catcher's mitt is not made for pop-ups). Players should not be too quick to call for the ball, and they must make sure it will land in their territory. With rules of priority, it's always clear what to do. If the shortstop calls for the ball anywhere in the infield, he gets it, and everyone else backs off.

8. Holding runners. As with second basemen, if there is an unforced player on second or third, the shortstop should see if the runner is going and should fake a throw to hold him on base before throwing to first. The shortstop's fake on this play, again, has to be the quickest of all, because he barely has time to get the ball to first as it is. Sometimes, all he will have time for is to give the runner a sharp, stern look. This is a good move to practice a few times. Have the shortstop fake a throw to third and then make a throw to first. Remember, he has to work on quickness or he will lose the runner on first.

9. Steals. The shortstop should take throws from the catcher on a steal attempt from first base. This must be practiced. The shortstop should straddle the back left side of the bag and bring the ball down very quickly to a spot 6 inches in front of the bag to make the tag. (See figure 5-7.) Remind your player that he doesn't have to stand on the bag. Often, kids think they need to have a foot on the bag, and this reduces their mobility. They should straddle the back left side of the bag, facing the catcher. They must understand that catching the ball, wherever it is, is more important than tagging

5-7. **TAGGING A RUNNER**

Straddle base, bend knees, block base with glove. Let runner slide into low glove.

the runner. Once the player catches the ball, his next move is to bring the glove down quickly to the runner's side of the base to tag the runner, who must slide.

THIRD BASE

Usually, in youth baseball, the fewest number of ground balls are hit to third base. In the pros, it's called the "hot corner," but not for youngsters. That's because the batters don't have enough bat speed, so they tend to hit more up the middle or to the right side. Coaches have a chance to use third base to try out different kids at infielding. It's also a place to put a kid who may be a bit weak defensively but whose bat is too good to leave out of the lineup.

Third base is a good position for a kid who has a decent glove, good arm, and good reflexes, but is too slow to play shortstop or second. A third baseman must have a good arm to reach first base on grounders and the ability to catch a throw from the catcher on runners stealing third. If the third baseman misses the throw, the runner can go home if the local rules allow it.

KEYS TO PLAYING THIRD BASE

1. Know the area. The third baseman, like the first baseman, should know where the sideline fence is for purposes of chasing down foul pop-ups or running after errant throws. For practice, you can throw some pop-ups close to the fence. Tell the third baseman to see where the ball is going, head in that direction, take a quick glance at where the fence or dugout is, adjust accordingly, and then look again at the ball. It feels very awkward at first to take your eye off the ball, but it's not so bad after practicing it a few times.

2. Play up. The third baseman should play in close, past the bag. Since the ball usually is not hit hard to third in Little League, grounders are often slow. Usually, I have the third baseman line up just behind the fringe of the infield grass. Have him back up a bit for better hitters. He has to learn to charge the slow dribbler. If it's slow enough, it can be picked up with one hand, but only if needed to beat the runner at first. The idea, as with fielding any grounder, is to scoop the ball from behind rather than snatch it from above. It will have less chance to roll under the hand.

3. Cutoff. As discussed earlier, the third baseman is never a cutoff. In the pros, the third baseman is the cutoff for plays at the plate from the left side of the outfield; on the smaller Little League fields, he is not needed. Coaches must be practical. The third

5-8. **THE HOT CORNER**

The defining move for third basemen. Concentrate on and time the ball, then dive and stab it. Knock it down, if that's all you can do.

baseman guards an important bag, and he should stay there. He doesn't go out for relays; the shortstop does that. On plays to home plate, the pitcher is my cutoff in youth baseball. If the pitcher is backing up third, the first baseman comes in if he is free. The third baseman's job is to guard third base, and that's it.

4. Dive for it! The essence of third base is diving for hot liners or grounders. (See figure 5-8.) The image of Brooks Robinson, perhaps the best defensive player who ever lived, diving left for hard shots and then popping up for an amazing throw to first is etched in the minds of fans everywhere. Tell your players that this is often what it takes. It's hard to practice, but it should be in their minds. By staying low, the fielder can dive at a hard grounder if needed to reach it. It's a tough play, but it may be the only chance to catch the ball.

5. Hold runners. As with other infielders, if there is an unforced player on second or third, the third baseman should see if the runner is going and perhaps fake a throw to hold him on base before he makes the throw to first.

OUTFIELD

In youth baseball, certainly at beginner and intermediate levels, left field is a very lonely position. Until players are about eleven or twelve, they usually don't get the bat around quickly enough—the pitchers are too fast. The ball is usually hit to right or center field. With fast pitchers, I always put my best outfielder in right field. If the pitcher is slower, then I put my strength in center field. The right fielder, in any event, needs to be a decent catcher and have the strongest arm in the outfield to get the ball to third base. Left field is a place to learn. There is not much action, not much pressure. Chapter three addressed some general defensive techniques and set forth practice drills for outfielders. A key idea with beginners is to practice using soft balls, like tennis balls or rubber balls. Cork-filled balls are also good. The child should catch the ball above eye level, palm facing outward. It is common for youth players to misjudge fly balls and to come in too far, so they should stand deeper than where they believe the ball will land. It's always easier to come in than it is to go back, and catching the ball while moving provides momentum for a good throw. Read the material in chapter three on catching fly balls for more information on this skill.

KEYS TO PLAYING OUTFIELD

1. Get under the ball. The main idea is to get quickly to the ball and get under it. Then get set to catch the ball and to make the transition to throw the ball. Also, on a ball over the head, the outfielder should turn and run, not back up (or try to run backwards).

2. Stance. The position of the outfielder is a comfortable stance, legs shoulder width apart, with the weight on the balls of feet and centered over the legs, so that the outfielder can move quickly in any direction. He must be ready to spring laterally very suddenly.

3. Fielding outfield grounders. If hit hard, these are among the toughest fielding plays to make in baseball. The fields that the kids play on are often not rolled in the springtime; the grass may be kept at varying lengths; there are often ruts, holes, rocks, or grass clumps. The ball can take wicked bounces.

Outfielders should break hard with the sound of the bat and charge a ground ball, even if hit at an infielder, since it could take a bad hop and get by. On a line drive that can't be caught, they should approach the ball from a distance that allows for a good bounce. If there are no other runners on base, outfielders may lower one knee to the ground. It's best if the knee barely touches the ground, so the fielder can come up quickly if the ball bounces wide. (See figure 5-9 on page 88.)

The transition from catching to throwing is not as important as it is in the infield. The fielder makes sure to stop the ball, getting the body in front of it, and gets a good grip to throw. Of course, with runners in scoring position, the outfielder needs to be

5-9. FIELDING OUTFIELD GROUNDERS

A major problem arises when a ball scoots by an outfielder. Try to get directly in front of it and block the path with the lowered leg. Move quickly since runners are looking to advance.

more aggressive to get the ball quickly into the infield. However, even then he should have the ball under control!

4. Where to throw. A brief summary follows for a base hit in front of the outfielder, or in other words, not a deep shot. I also review the concepts of throwing ahead of the lead runner and hitting the cutoff in detail in chapter three.

    i. No one on. Get the ball toward second base. The outfielder should hit the cutoff, the shortstop, or the second baseman, depending on which side of the field he is on. The cutoff should be standing about 15 to 25 feet in front of the base.

    ii. Man on first. Throw the ball toward third base. Make sure to hit the cutoff, the shortstop.

    iii. Men on first and second. Throw home toward the cutoff in the middle of the infield. It should be the pitcher or first baseman. The pitcher will cut off the ball if the runner on second stops at third.

    iv. Man on second or men on second and third. The runner on second is the lead runner, and it's the same as number three, except now the batter will look to go to second, so the cutoff has to keep an eye on him.

    v. Man on third. Same as number one. As far as the outfield is concerned, there is nobody on, since the runner on third will score by the time the outfielder has the ball.

    vi. Bases loaded. Same as number three. The runner on third will score; it's the runner on second you want to stop; he is the lead runner for outfield purposes.

5. Fielding balls hit to the fence. If the ball is hit over the outfielder's head or through the gap to the fence, he should get it as fast as he can. It will be a long throw, so the shortstop or the second baseman may have to come out to help. The outfielder should not look around or hesitate. He is too far away to throw anybody out, so he should just quickly get the ball to the relay and let that player make the throw. If there is no one on, the throw should be toward third base since the batter will likely get to second base. If there is a runner on first, he is a definite scoring threat, and the throw must head toward home since he will easily get to third (unless he is quite slow). Remember, it's important to have general rules, and it's also important to know that there are exceptions. Players must understand the concepts and generally follow them, but they may need to improvise during the game.

6. Backing up steals. On a throw from the catcher to second base during a steal, the center fielder backs up second base. Similarly, on such a throw to third base, the left fielder backs up third base. The left fielder may not get many hits in his direction, but there will be throws from the catcher to third, and many will get past the third baseman. On the pitch, the left fielder should hold his position until the ball passes the batter, and then get ready to break toward the third base foul line, toward a point about 20 feet behind third base. If the throw is wild, the left fielder must head where the ball is heading. He should not get too close to the third baseman, otherwise the ball could get by.

7. Pop-ups and tagging up. Remember that runners tag up on fly balls that outfielders catch. An outfielder can't stand there gleaming over a great catch—he must get the ball to the base in front of the lead runner.

PITCHER

Last, but certainly not least is the pitcher I've said several times that the essence, the joy, of baseball is hitting, and it surely is, but winning games at any level of baseball is generally all about pitching. Whether an eight year old or a big leaguer, a good pitcher is simply more valuable than anything else. This is just a fact of life in baseball. Championships are won at every level with good pitching.

Hitting is for everybody, because everybody is, and can be, a hitter. Pitching, however, certainly at youth levels, is pretty much done by the most gifted athletes. Some kids just have a knack for getting the ball over the plate. Others can throw hard, (*heat* as it's called,) and all they need are innings (or perhaps a few years) of experience and some better tech-

89

5-10. THE PITCHER

Games are won with pitching heat and control.

niques to gain control. A few rare ones have both control and speed at an early age, and their teams will nearly always win with them on the mound. (See figure 5-10.)

Anyone who can throw reasonably hard should be given opportunities and time to develop as a pitcher, since the fastball is the cornerstone of pitching. Control comes with time for many kids. Others have good control, but need to grow to get arm strength and speed. I urge coaches at beginner levels to give lots of kids the chance. And if they don't have skill sufficient for a game, let every kid pitch a dozen or so balls at practice. I've seen so many kids over the years who never got a chance suddenly show good stuff. It only takes a few minutes at practice to let two kids at a time throw to each other, perhaps with a parent supervising.

If you want to evaluate a child's pitching ability, have him pitch a dozen to you and see how many strikes he throws and whether he throws hard. Most pitches should be from quite close. At intermediate levels, kids will pitch about 45 miles per hour, picking up to about 55 or so miles per hour by eleven to twelve years old. The best twelve-year-old pitchers in the world, seen at the Little League World Series, can throw pitches nearly 80 miles per hour.

ARM BURNOUT

You will know pretty quickly if a player is a potential pitcher. However, this is one point where I caution against too much practice. The shoulder and elbow muscles and tendons are placed under much stress when throwing a ball, and it is simply scandalous how many kids burn out their arms in Little League-level play.

Little League pitching rules limit pitchers twelve years of age and under to six innings per week and six innings per game. If a pitcher pitches in three or fewer innings, one day of rest is required before pitching again. If a pitcher pitches in four or more innings, three days of rest are required. The number of innings allowed is increased for older age groups. Optional regulations for leagues taking part in the 2006 Little League Pitch Count Pilot Program will limit the number of actual pitches thrown by a pitcher in a day, regardless of the number of innings pitched, based on the pitcher's age. Once eleven to twelve year olds reach eighty-five pitches (seventy-five pitches if under eleven years old), they may not pitch to another batter, and must then have four days of rest. For forty-one to sixty pitches, required rest is three days; and for twenty-one to forty pitches, it's two days. Under twenty-one pitches requires one day of rest.

But, good pitchers not only pitch at games and at practice, they are often called on by their friends to pitch in pick-up games. Some kids will play on two teams and pitch for both. Big league pitchers get four days of rest, yet kids at play often pitch nearly every day. Don't let that happen. As a parent, set rules and enforce them. This is especially true during the first weeks of the season. Kids should never throw on less than two days' rest, and never pitch more than three innings. Several years ago, the American Sports Medicine Institute surveyed coaches and doctors and found that eleven- to twelve-year-old pitchers should throw no more than sixty-eight pitches and get two days' rest. Younger kids should pitch no more than fifty pitches. During the season, ensure that a pitcher's arm gets rested. Above all, don't play or practice pitching every day. You don't want too many hard throws a day, and a kid should never throw hard until he has a few dozen soft throws to warm up.

THE FUNDAMENTALS OF PITCHING

Assuming you have a budding pitcher, what do you need to know about style? I'll discuss here the elements of a pitch, but the thing to start talking about right away is consistency. A good pitcher is a robot on the mound, throwing pretty much with the same movement every pitch. Your players must understand this immediately.

Pitching form is *not* a combination of different moves, but one continuous, smooth, and explosive action. The following section breaks down pitching into its parts, but the movement is ultimately one fluid motion. Coaches need to guard against their pitchers losing the forest for the trees.

1. The grip. For a basic four-seam fastball, place the first and middle fingers on the top of the ball, crossing the threads. The thumb goes on the left side of the ball, and

5-11. **FOUR-SEAM FASTBALL GRIP**

Fingertips over seam, ball not too deep into palm.

ring and pinkie fingers on the right, cradling the ball. The two top fingers should be fairly close together. The pitcher holds the ball with the fingers; the ball does not touch the palm, and there should be a space in the thumb pocket. (See figure 5-11.) The grip should be fairly loose, which allows for the wrist flick to fully deliver the power and velocity generated from the rest of the body.

2. Address the batter. Pitchers in Little League usually have a small mound with a rectangular-shaped rubber pad on top of it. Tell your child (if righty, opposite for lefty) to step on the rubber with the right foot, toes slightly overhanging the rubber, and face the batter. Don't look at the batter; look only at the catcher's mitt. Hands can be up, or down at the side. The left foot is even with or slightly behind the right foot, to the left side of the rubber. The pitcher should stand on the *same spot* on the rubber each time. Most kids want to lean forward a bit, but the key is to be comfortable. If there is no rubber, have a pitcher draw a box in the dirt or make some mark. Pitchers must always be thinking about consistency.

You want the pitching style to look the same each time. Talk about this idea. Talk about gracefulness. Also talk about power. But, control arises from consistent form, and you want the pitcher to be very mechanical in form. (See figure 5-12 on pages 94–95.)

Some pitchers address the batter from a set or stretch position. This approach essentially eliminates the Rocker explained in number three. He starts with his back foot astride the front of the rubber, standing sideways to the batter. It adds to control, but detracts from power by eliminating the rocking motion and reducing the Pivot and Crane (explained in number four) some. You might consider it for a hardball thrower who has control issues.

3. The Rocker. This is also called the windup, but is essentially a rocking motion. Step or rock the left foot back a half step, shifting just enough weight to get the rocking momentum. The hands are together and up, to chest height, perhaps higher, then they drop a bit to the abdomen area, and finally come to a stop.

4. The Pivot and Crane. After the pitcher rocks back, he turns or pivots his right foot, placing it firmly astride (still touching) the rubber. He then lifts his left leg to *at least* a 90 degree angle at the knee in a balanced posture; shoulders are level. Lifting the leg resembles a crane (a large bird) standing on one leg. The left leg should be just over the space to the left of the right foot, not leaning toward home, and not swept back toward second base. A good drill for pitchers to practice is to stop in this position to make sure they are balanced and able to hold the posture for some time.

Most pros, when they crane, are cocking and gathering their power. They lift their knee at least waist high, and sometimes chest high. This adds power, but it can affect control for a youngster. Some kids get into the bad habit of merely sweeping their left foot back toward second base, rather than lifting it; that must be corrected at once. The idea is to load up power comfortably, raising the leg to a height that feels good. After time and experience, pitchers can crane higher for more power. But they must get the control first.

At the peak of the crane, the pitcher separates his hands and reaches back with his right (pitching) hand toward second base, extending it straight back and downward. This promotes full extension early in the pitch and prevents erratic movement at that critical moment. If the arm drifts off to first or third base slightly, it can throw off the pitch. One professional pitcher told me he liked to reach toward his back pocket with the ball, just to start at the same point each time. Chapter three discusses this idea of extending the arm when throwing as a method to correct "arm throwing." The front elbow faces home.

5. The Drive. At this point the pitcher rocks forward again, driving toward the batter. He drives hard and low with the back leg for power, rolling the drive foot counterclockwise on the ground, and then rhythmically strides or kicks the front leg down, then out. It's important for the pitcher to feel the back or driving foot pushing off the end of the rubber. Much power can be added from the back foot.

6. Stay closed. *Staying closed* means that until the stride foot lands, the front elbow, shoulders, and throwing arm stay aligned to the plate. The opposite is *flying open*, where the upper body, particularly the shoulders, opens up, turning with the stride.

5-12. **SIX PARTS OF THE PITCH.**

Part 1: Address the batter. Start from same spot and position, consistency is key. Grip ball with the fingers, away from the palm. Take a breath.

Part 2: The Rocker. Step and rock the body back, then step to front of the rubber, slowly turning right foot.

Part 3: The Crane. Lift front knee straight up while gathering and loading power.

Part 4: The Kick. Reach straight back with ball, keep shoulder and hips closed, stride front leg down and out toward batter.

Part 5: The Drive and "open the door." Plant the front foot, extend the throwing arm, keep the elbow up, throw over the top, open up the hips, and fire away.

Part 6: The Follow-Through. Follow through fully and gracefully. Stay low, let the drive foot naturally. Swing forward to regain balance, and prepare for a play.

This deprives the pitcher of the torque from the leg drive and leaves him only with the power from the shoulder and arm muscles. Flying open is a natural result of the stride, and so staying closed is a skill that has to be learned.

Drill to Stay Closed. Have the pitcher go through the pitching motion in front of a mirror. He should concentrate on the lead elbow and shoulder staying aligned to the plate. The front hip opens a bit upon planting the stride foot, but the lead elbow and front shoulder stay aligned and closed. The pitcher tightens the abdominal muscles to keep his upper body closed.

6. Point, plant, and "open the door." The front or kick foot shoots down and out toward home and should land on the left side of an imaginary line from the back foot to the middle of the plate, toes pointed toward home or bent inward no more than 10 to 15 degrees. For maximum power, the stretch should be fairly long, maybe 80 to 90 percent of the length of the pitcher's height. A long stretch brings the body's center of gravity down, so the pitch comes down, too. Low and outside pitches are the best pitches. The foot should land squarely, as flat as possible, trying not to jerk the body too much. A pitcher should try to land the foot at the same spot every pitch. At that moment, "he opens the door." The left foot lands and the hip opens with the planting of the foot; then the left shoulder and left arm are like a door, opening up explosively with the pitch. The upper torso rotates powerfully, providing torque and arm speed.

Often, pitchers don't open up enough, stepping to the right (righty pitcher) rather than left side of the imaginary line from the back foot to the middle of the plate. Or they land with that foot pointing toward third base, and the leg interferes with the follow-through. Others open up too soon and end up over-rotating, losing power and control.

I teach my pitchers to perceive that they are driving their left shoulder and hip at the batter, staying closed, and then at the end of the stride, they open it up and powerfully "swing the door." The left foot should point to the plate when it lands and not come down at an angle to the plate. Also, the left foot should come down hard, pulling the pitcher into a complete follow-through. Al Santorini was probably the best high school pitcher New Jersey ever had and pitched for a good number of years in the pros. Al, himself a Little League coach in the 1990s, told me that very few coaches realize the importance of landing hard with the stretch foot.

7. Come over the top. The delivery should be over the top, arm and ball as high as possible, with the elbow leading the forearm forward. To avoid sidearm throws, it is of greatest importance to keep the elbow up, higher than the shoulder. Kids sometimes go to sidearm when they are tired or because they feel it gives more control. Sure, we've all seen good sidearm pitchers. Bret Saberhagen was one of the best relievers in the game in the early 1980s, and he threw sidearm/underhanded. But be sure to encourage your players to come over the top, or at least at a three-quarter (270 degree) angle. This produces a more powerful pitch, and it's better for longevity of the arm, since the motion is not as herky-jerky as the sidearm throw.

8. The release. The throwing arm should be extended and driven forward by the snap of the hip, shoulder, elbow, and wrist. The body is brought down hard with the front foot. The ball is released as high as possible and as close to the batter as possible. Most release points are at a point just past the tip of the pitcher's cap.

9. The follow-through. As a natural consequence of forward and downward rotation, the pitching hand follows through the ball toward the ground. A follow-through is the result of a good drive and a good stretch; it should happen automatically because of forward momentum. If a player has to try to follow through, he just doesn't have enough forward momentum. The pitcher snaps his wrist downward, making the ball spin, but also causing the follow-through. Lack of follow-through is a good sign that the wrist is not snapping.

96

OTHER KEYS TO PITCHING

At the younger ages, the strategy is simple—just get the ball over the plate. The pitcher who gives up the most walks will lose. At the older ages, you can begin to discuss some strategy.

1. Take your time. Too often, kids rush from one pitch to the next. They need to develop a rhythm, and they need to focus on concentration. When you start seeing high pitches, it's a good time to slow the pitcher down.

2. Hit the glove. The catcher's glove is the whole world to the pitcher. He should block everything out except thinking about the glove and trying to hit it. In time, as he gains control, the pitcher should think about the corners of the glove. He must focus on the catcher's glove at all times and during every part of the pitch. It's not that he aims at the glove; it's just that it is all he should see.

3. Get in front of the batter. This means having more strikes than balls in the count. The first strike is important. If a pitcher has two strikes and no or one ball, he should rear back and fire some heat. He shouldn't let a batter beat him when he is ahead. Pitchers can afford to give up some control in favor of heat when they are ahead in the count.

4. Know the batters. If a batter won't swing, throw easy strikes. Fire heat at the good hitters.

5. Cover first base. If a ball is hit to the pitcher's left side, the pitcher must always break to cover first base. If he is not needed, he can stop. On a bunt or a slow roller, the pitcher should charge the ball, but defer to the catcher if he gets to it at the same time, since the catcher will have the better angle for a throw.

6. Cutoff. If the lead runner is on first base, the pitcher backs up third. If the lead runner is on second, the pitcher is the cutoff at the plate. On a passed ball or wild pitch with a runner on third, the pitcher covers the plate.

7. Direct the action. Since the pitcher has the best view of the action on a hit ball, he should take charge on helping fielders with where to throw the ball.

PITCHING FROM THE STRETCH

The advent of larger field dimensions in some youth leagues and rules that allow runners to steal at any time have required pitchers to shorten their windups and to pitch

05

from the stretch. This is a very simple movement by which the pitcher stands sideways in front of the rubber (his back foot must touch the rubber) and simply steps toward home with the pitch, driving the body with the rear foot. (See figure 5-13.) The motion reduces the power of the pitch somewhat, since there is no windup, and the lead foot does not kick up very high; it's more of a slide step toward the batter. When pitching from the stretch, there is usually a runner on base, and the pitcher must keep an eye on the runner until just before the stride to keep him close to the base.

TYPES OF PITCHES

As noted earlier, the *fastball* is the bread and butter of pitching. (The great professional pitchers can throw rising fastballs—an extremely difficult pitch to hit with a bat moving in a downward arc.) At young ages, the fastball is pretty much the only pitch used. It's just a hard, straight pitch. And it's the easiest pitch to control. If the ball is gripped across the seams as in figure 5-11 (on page 92), called a *four-seam fastball*, it will go straight, and even rise a bit as the pitcher becomes stronger. The other way to throw a fastball, and probably better for the smaller hands in youth baseball, is to place the index and middle fingers across the area where the seams are closest together, placing the fingers perpendicular to the seams, called a *two-seamer*. (See figure 5-14 A on page 99.) This will cause the ball to sink a bit, but is harder to control.

The *curveball* (see figure 5-14 B) is the second most popular pitch, but kids rarely throw it before high school. Coaches don't know how to teach the curveball, and that's good because it's tougher on the arm than a fastball if it is thrown wrong. The main idea is to throw more with the middle finger, lined up astride a seam, and to snap and

5-13. **PITCHING FROM THE STRETCH**

To speed up the delivery and allow less time for a runner to steal, eliminate the windup and go directly to a stride and drive.

turn the wrist sharply, giving the ball a sideways spin. The throw is a bit "short-armed," and as the wrist snaps, it turns in toward the body. It is essential to keep the elbow up. You can have pitchers try it, but don't concentrate on it.

Other pitches are *sliders, split-finger fastballs, knuckleballs,* and *change-ups.*

The *change-up* is an interesting pitch and is the only other pitch I recommend teaching to kids in grade school. (See figure 5-14 C.) The pitcher's arm moves as if for a fastball, but the unique grip slows it down, and thus *changes* the ball's speed. The change-up needs to be thrown a lot before it can be used effectively. The change-up is

5-14. **OTHER PITCHES**

A: Two-seam fastball.

B: Curveball.

C: Change-up.

thrown just like a fastball, so that the batter does not know it's coming, but the grip is wholly different. Instead of being out on the fingers, the ball is stuffed back into the palm with two or three fingers loose on top of the ball. The wrist snap is not used, and the ball is launched stiff-wristed, just with centrifugal force. The change-up is an important pitch to have along with a good fastball.

As to the others, especially curveballs, don't encourage your child to learn these until high school. He'll kill his arm trying to learn them too early. Besides, some local rules forbid "funny" pitches.

COACHING TEE-BALL

06

When I started coaching thirty years ago, kids started playing organized ball at age nine. Every five years or so, I'd hear about kids starting a year earlier. Now they start at four to five years old. Is three next? Most Tee-Ball leagues include ages five to six.

When Tee-Ball leagues first started to spring up, I recall coaches for the older kids complaining that it was too young to start playing organized ball. Many coaches said hitting a ball off a batting tee taught kids to swing improperly by not striding into a moving ball. Others worried about injuries, since some kids were slow to get their gloves up, or just could not catch. I once saw a kid throw the ball at a runner to get him out.

Well, it's still baseball! It's the first experience with baseball for most kids. Kids love it, and it's here to stay. Over two million kids play Tee-Ball each year. I had a lot of fun recently helping out my granddaughter's team.

IT IS BASEBALL

I placed this chapter subsequent to the various other chapters on skills and positions because Tee-Ball is indeed baseball, and most of what is contained in the other chapters applies to five year olds as well as to twelve year olds. The rules are modified to promote safety, to accommodate skill level, and to focus on having fun. Here are some of the differences:

1. Balls are not pitched. Balls are hit from the tip of an adjustable, rubber batting tee that is placed on home plate. The tee can be adjusted to the batter's height and should be about even with the batter's waist. The coach places the ball on top of the tee, and the batter stands in the batter's box, in normal batting position, and hits the ball onto the field of play. The pitcher and catcher still stand near their positions to play defense. Coaches should ensure the catcher stands away from the batter in case the bat is thrown.

Coaches in some leagues will try to pitch to kids late in the season or to kids six years old or older. After a few missed swings, the tee is brought to the plate and the kid will hit off the tee. I've seen leagues try to have kids pitch to each other, but it's usually not successful, and I believe it's far too early to tax a kid's arm.

2. There are no strikes called. Players swing until they hit the ball into fair play. Once a ball is hit, the batter advances to first base and regular baseball rules apply. Some leagues limit the number of bases that may be taken on a hit. This also limits the amount of throwing kids have to do, which can get a bit crazy, and it keeps play much safer for all. No base stealing is allowed, even on a passed ball when coaches are pitching.

3. All players take the field when on defense. Players rotate each inning to a different position to gain experience with all positions. Defensive players are usually not allowed to crowd the plate, for obvious safety reasons. Some leagues place a lime arc at a 40-foot radius from home plate; players are not allowed inside that arc.

4. All players bat in order. This means no one is ever out of the game. Coaches roam the field giving instructions.

5. Scores usually are not kept. No winners or losers, no standings. Everyone gets a trophy at the end of the season. (But kids can count, and they will make it known if they think they won).

6. Usually every player gets to bat every inning. But some leagues opt for the three-out rule. An inning can last forever. Games are usually limited by time to ninety minutes; some clubs play four-inning games.

7. Putouts are called. These include catching a pop-up and tagging or throwing a runner out. Some leagues don't do this, but the game makes less sense to the kids without outs. Even when a kid is called out, everyone cheers about his good contact with the ball, so it's not so bad to be called out.

8. Bats are shorter. Bat length is generally 25 to 26 inches and from 17 to 20 ounces in weight. The ball is a bit softer than a standard baseball; it's 9 inches around, about 4½ ounces in weight.

TALKING BASEBALL

Don't assume the kids know anything about baseball, because they will know little. At the first practices, get the team together and talk baseball a bit. Ask who their favorite team or player is and how the team is doing. Talk about the jargon of baseball. Have a list of words like strike, foul, pop-up, grounder, and walk. Make it fun. Ask if any player knows what each word means. Do ten new words at each practice. Go over the various positions and field terms: right field, shortstop, foul territory. Talk a bit about the rules. Not too much at first. Use the glossary in this book to develop your word lists.

SKILLS

As noted earlier, Tee-Ball is baseball, and so all skills are similar and should be coached. Obviously, the degree of coordination, interest, ability to learn, and concentration of a five year old is much different than that of a ten year old. It's important to keep things fun and simple, and to try to communicate on a level a very young child will understand. Much of the material in this book distinguishes beginners from advanced-level play; obviously, the beginner-level instructions apply to Tee-Ball.

Getting parents involved is very important in Tee-Ball. I would, however, try to ensure that parents do not coach their own children too much.

BATTING

Well, we started with hitting in this book and will do so with Tee-Ball also. Here are some tips. (See figure 6-1.)

1. Stance. Show a kid the proper stance right away. Use the Circle Stance Drill explained in chapter two on page 23 and talk about each part of the stance. Tell players to "look like a hitter," and then use this phrase every time they lapse into a poor stance at the plate.

2. Swing. Kids will tend to hit a Tee-Ball stiff-legged, so tell them to take a small stride step into the ball (pushing off the back foot, "squashing the bug"). Swinging level and

6-1. TEE-BALL

Focus on a good stance, stride, and hitting the middle of the ball.

thrusting the hands toward the ball are also keys at this level. Use a marker to paint a dime-sized spot on the ball and tell them to hit the spot. Have them practice dropping the bat, not throwing it, after they hit. Make this something important because kids will develop the bad habit of throwing the bat, and it needs to be stopped early.

3. Running. Once they hit, they need to know where to go. I once told a kid to run around the bases, and he did just that, running to first and making a circle around the bag. Don't assume they know what to do. Line them up at home plate and have them run to each base. Remind them to run *through* (or past) first base. Then start the next kid, and have the runner on first go to second, and so forth.

FIELDING

1. Grounders. The instructions in chapter three apply at all levels. Talk about stance: getting the glove low, head up; bending the knees, not so much the waist; and scooping the ball up. Start with a rubber or tennis ball and have the kids leave their gloves on the bench at first. Go over proper position: hands cupped and together, pinkies close to each other, ready to scoop. Don't add difficulty until they are ready for it. If you have a smooth surface nearby, use it. Throw balls with one hop and make it easy.

2. Pop-ups. Again, start by having a catch with a rubber ball and add distance only when it makes sense. A good drill for beginners is to cut out the bottom of a gallon milk container, and have the kids use it to catch pop-ups. Throw—don't bat—the ball to them so that it comes at a height and spot that allows them to catch. Don't go to a hard ball until they can handle it.

3. Throwing. A lot of initial practice time should be having a catch. Tell parents to do it at home. Work on the throwing stance. Watch their feet and make sure they push off with the foot on the same side they throw on (right foot for righties). Make sure they start sideways with the glove shoulder pointing at the target, then reach back with the throwing arm, and throw with elbow and hands high, arm extended. Follow through by pivoting on the opposite foot (left foot for righties). A fun drill is the Target Practice Drill explained in chapter three on page 52.

PITCHING

I have nothing to say about pitching at the Tee-Ball level, except *don't do it*. Don't allow your child to pitch even if the coach wants him to do so. Save his arm. However, kids do stand in the pitching area to play defense, and they get a lot of balls hit into this area.

PRACTICES

Chapter seven will cover in detail how to run a practice. Much of it will apply to Tee-Ball.

1. Practice plan. Use the model practice plan form at the end of chapter seven and plan out your practices. Always begin with a warm-up for ten minutes. Talk baseball for ten minutes, go over terminology, and tell the kids and parents the plan for the day. Then break out into stations. One group can hit off the tee; a second group can work on batting form, stance, and swing. A third group can have a catch, emphasizing throwing form. Another group can work on grounders, adding in a throw to first base at some point. Rotate the kids to each station after ten to fifteen minutes. It's important to reserve time for a scrimmage and for team dynamics so the kids can see the skills in live baseball action. Coaches should stay on the field and should freely stop play to talk about what the kids did and what should have occurred. Place kids into the proper location at each position and keep reminding them to be there.

2. Involve parents. I'm being repetitious, but this is critical to how much the kids will learn, and how much fun the season will be for all. Use parents, even if it's just to have an easy catch with someone else's kid. Have them monitor a station, retrieve balls, hand out water, and keep the kids occupied and focused.

SAFETY FIRST

Don't ever forget the age of your kids in Tee-Ball. They often are unaware of their surroundings or the risks involved.

1. Don't let players swing the bat except in a designated area, such as the batter's box during a game or a batting area during practice. Don't allow swinging at any other time or place. Baseball bats are hard and can seriously injure a player. Remind players to stay away from designated areas when someone is swinging the bat. Keep all the bats in one place, and don't allow kids to grab them until they are to be used.

2. Players can't throw bats. I mentioned this previously, and it's worth repeating. Draw a box in the dirt behind the batter, near the corner of the batter's box, and tell batters to always drop the bat near that spot.

3. Make great use of rubber balls. Practice with them exclusively for weeks until the kids have some decent form and confidence in catching.

4. Keep the kids together, and don't let anyone go to a snack stand without an adult. Keep them in the dugout when not playing.

5. Keep infielders well behind the 40-foot circle when on defense. It's there for their protection.

SUMMARY

The purpose of Tee-Ball is to learn the great game of baseball. Yes, it's about fun, and it's about helping little kids build a good self-image through positive reinforcement. A coach should not foster any competitiveness and should not tolerate any parental stress on a child's performance. By the same token, the kids need to learn basics, terminology, good form, hustle, and teamwork. So keep it a teaching experience and gently insist on a reasonable level of discipline. It can be, and must be, a wonderful coaching experience and a great opportunity to make good friends—parents and kids.

RUNNING A PRACTICE

I've watched maybe a hundred different teams at practice over my thirty years of coaching. Many involved a coach pitching to a batter, with the rest of the team swatting flies or daydreaming in the outfield, then after an hour or so they would switch gears, and the coach would hit balls to his players. The problem with this picture is that most of the kids are standing around 95 percent of the time doing nothing. Another problem is that the coach is not able to closely observe and correct his players' form and performance since he so involved in pitching or hitting. The solution to both problems is a plan that involves all kids in continuous action and requires getting at least several parents to help you implement that plan.

START EARLY

The first job is to communicate with your team, seek some help, make a few suggestions, and set the rules. At least a month before your first practice, you should get the word out to your team. The local ball club or association will give you a list of players and their addresses, hopefully including e-mail addresses. Write the parents a letter; a sample is given below. Tell parents that the season will go much better if players show up in decent shape. Baseball doesn't require the endurance of most other sports, but it does require strength, quickness, and agility. I feel it's best, particularly at the intermediate levels of eight to ten years old, to suggest that players come to practices able to run a half-dozen 30-yard wind sprints and able to do ten to twenty pushups. Younger kids won't have the upper body strength, but they can get started. Have them do what they can, and then strive for *just one more!* This means they should work at least every other day to get up to this level. We'll review further, but pushups are *great* for hitting baseballs hard.

Players and parents also need to know that practices are important and that being on time is key for them and for the team. The game schedule, practice schedule, and starting and ending times all should be communicated when available so parents can begin arranging for transportation.

You should communicate that you welcome help. At least two or three assistant coaches are needed. Team parents are needed to help with incidentals, such as uniforms, candy drives, and car pools. Don't be afraid to ask for help! A sample letter to parents follows.

Dear Parent/Guardian,

Welcome to the (Name) Baseball program. Our season starts in about a month, and I'd like to go over a few things that will help us get off to a great start!

Practices will start on (Date). We will practice every Tuesday evening and Saturday morning until the first game, currently scheduled for (Date). Practices are for two hours, from 5:30 to 7:30 P.M. Tuesday and from 9:30 to 11:30 A.M. Saturday. It's important that your child arrives on time (a few minutes early is fine) and is picked up on time.

Baseball shoes and a glove are required at practices and games. Children should bring water. Early in the season, our practices may occur during cool periods, so make sure kids are dressed warmly. They can always take off sweat-shirts or jackets if it warms up.

Our games will generally be on Tuesday evenings and Saturday mornings, and the starting time may vary a bit. I'll get a detailed schedule out as soon as possible. Practices during the season will vary, and we'll discuss this further when we meet. Please send me your e-mail address if you received this by regular mail to facilitate quick communication. My e-mail is (Your Address).

It would be very helpful to your child to do some mild conditioning before the season starts, so that initial practices are not too tiring. Jogging, wind sprints (six for 30 yards each—remember to warm up first!), and push-ups are very helpful (build up to about fifteen, or whatever he can do). On a nice day, you may want to encourage your child to have a catch to loosen up his arm.

I encourage parental involvement, and I need a few assistant coaches. Don't worry about experience; we can all learn as we go. There is a great book called *Coaching Youth Baseball: A Guide for Parents and Coaches*, by John P. McCarthy, and I recommend you obtain it. I also need a team parent or two to help organize things. If you are interested, give me a call or see me at the first practice.

My philosophy is to help your child learn the skills and fundamentals, become a better player, and have fun with the great game of baseball. Most kids do not go on to play at advanced levels, but if they learn the basics, they will enjoy the game for many years. Every child will play in every game (or state your league's rule about minimum playing time). Those who work harder may get some additional playing time, but they must earn it! Winning is fun, but it is not important—and not nearly as important as making this a positive learning experience.

I hope you will keep this in mind when rooting for the team or your child at games. It's helpful to praise good effort, but it's not helpful to give specific instructions to your child during play (that's my role) or to comment on umpire calls (they are learning, too). I will not allow criticism from parents or other players.

It is most helpful for parents to work with their children at home to improve skills. Have a catch, throw some pitches, and perhaps try the batting cage located at (Address). Practice definitely leads to improvement, and more is always better! Players are expected to make all practices and games, barring illness or another very important event.

Of course, if your schedule does not permit more, you have already taken a big step by allowing your child to be involved and by providing transportation. Welcome aboard!

Best Regards,

Coach (Your Name)
Phone, e-mail, address

PRACTICE TIME

Unfortunately, as a coach, you probably won't get as much practice time as you want or need. There are often more teams than fields. Early in the season, there is not much daylight and plenty of April showers. Teams customarily practice a couple of times a week at best. An enterprising coach can find a way to get in more practices, but it's not the rule.

The best practice condition is on a regulation field with smoothed-out dirt surfaces. But any open field will do for batting, pitching, and outfield practice. A parking lot is fine for infield practice. If your club doesn't have its own, a trip to the local batting cage is an excellent alternative to a rained-out practice. Videotape the kids batting, pitching, and fielding, then plan an evening at someone's house to view the tapes, maybe with some pizza.

There are many ways to enrich a practice schedule, even if you just urge Mom, Dad, or a big brother or sister to spend thirty minutes having a catch. Advise them to throw some grounders and pop-ups (throw left, right, then deep) or to work on batting form. The No-Pitch Drill, described in chapter two on page 34, is a great form drill and requires no special area, just a net or link fence to hit balls against. The more you get your players drilling their skills, the better your team will be. It's the surest thing about any sport! A coach must find creative ways to get players more practice time. Sure, you may not be able to spend every night on baseball, but that's where parents and assistant coaches come in.

There are several key objectives to consider for each practice plan. Their relative importance will vary as you get further into the season and may also vary depending on what age group you work with. These concepts are always important and should be part of your plan for each practice.

SET YOUR PRACTICE GOALS

Baseball practices typically last two hours, depending on the day of the week and amount of daylight. The five goals reviewed below should be considered each time you prepare a practice plan. (I'll get to what a practice plan looks like a bit later.)

In a two-hour practice, I devote ten minutes to chatter and water breaks; ten to twenty minutes to conditioning; sixty minutes to batting practice; thirty minutes to defensive skills development; and thirty minutes to team dynamics. Doesn't add up? It does if you can do a few things at the same time! In fact, if you have a lot of parent-coaches helping out, you can seemingly double these time frames.

Early in the season, you should spend a bit more time on conditioning, speed, agility drills, and batting. Later in the season, spend more time on specialty drills for refinements such as cutoffs, bunts, pick-offs, and rundowns. Let's look at each goal.

GOAL ONE: GET THE PLAYERS IN SHAPE

Frankly, it doesn't take much to get grade-school or high-school kids into shape, and there is just no excuse when they aren't. Baseball does not require much endurance, but a lot of improvement can come from some strength training, speed drills, and agility drills. The worst mistake is to assume that kids will get themselves into shape. Baseball coaches tend to underestimate the value of conditioning, but stronger kids hit longer balls. Even if you only get your kids to double the number of push-ups they can do, they will be better hitters.

Warming Up

Make sure players warm up before practice. A few laps around the field at a slow pace should make them break a sweat and warm up major leg muscles. Of special concern early in the season are the large muscles high on the inner thigh and in the groin area. Most ballplayers have experienced strains in these areas, usually while running to first base, and they can take weeks to heal. Tell your players that muscles are like bubble gum—unless they stretch slowly, they will tear. After stretching, the kids should pair up and have a catch to loosen their arms and elbows. Tell them to get there a few minutes early each time to warm up before practice.

Don't expect that players will warm up sufficiently on their own. They should be told to stretch out on their own before practice, but get the team together to do it more. Players get hurt too easily when they're not loose, and you need to see that it gets done.

Start the team off with what I call the Quick Cali Set: twenty jumping jacks, ten push-ups, fifteen half sit-ups, and twenty trunk turns.

Then do a few from the Leg Stretch Set. Leg stretches should be done smoothly without jerking or straining. A few good ones are listed below. (See figure 7-1 on page 112.)

1. Butterfly Groin. One of the best stretches is to sit on the ground and place the soles of the sneakers together. Then gently pull the feet in close for fifteen seconds, relax, then pull in again. Do three to four times.

2. Thigh Stretch. The player stands with legs outstretched sideways and leans to one side, bending that knee, to stretch the opposite thigh muscle.

3. Toe-Hand. Lie on the back with arms stretched outward, on the ground. Alternately, bring each foot up and over to the opposite hand.

4. Hurdler. Sit on the ground with one leg forward and one bent inward. Touch the forward toe. Reverse legs and repeat.

5. Standing Quadriceps. Standing on one leg, lift the other foot from behind to touch the buttocks. Do a half dozen for each leg.

6. Supine Hamstring. Lying on the back with hands behind one knee, pull the leg as straight-legged as possible to the chest. Repeat with the other leg. No jerking movements, and no bobbing up and down.

7. Achilles and Calf Stretch. Place one foot a step in front of the other. Lean forward and bend the front leg, stretching the lower part of the back leg. Switch legs.

7-1. **STRETCHES AND STRENGTHENERS**

A: Toe Touches. Stand with legs crossed and touch as low as you can. Don't stretch too hard, hold for fifteen seconds, and then reverse legs.

B: Butterfly. Sit with soles of feet together and gently pull feet closer to body. Feel inside thigh muscles stretch.

C: Thigh Stretch. Standing with legs outstretched, lean to one side, bending that knee, stretching the opposite thigh muscle.

D: Push-Ups. Still the best exercise there is for wrist and forearm strength. Great for getting an edge on hitting power.

Any player or the team captain, if you have one, can lead exercises; he can start this part of the practice while you are getting organized or checking to see who is there and talking to coaches or parents. Monitor your players. Evaluate the temperature at all times when doing conditioning and make sure none of the players gets heat exhaustion, especially late in the season when it's hot.

Don't overwork players. Some coaches have kids running all the time, all season long. The players are young, but there are limits even for the young. Conditioning is less necessary for baseball than for other sports, so focus on the stretches.

By the same token, there can be periods when players are just standing around. I believe that push-ups are the best single exercise to build upper body strength in kids (along with sit-ups). Hand out sets of ten to twenty push-ups or sit-ups freely. Tell the kids that it will help them hit harder.

Another great strength enhancer to use at practice is what I call the *wrist machine*. It's simply a 2-foot section of broom handle or thick pipe with a 4-foot length of clothesline attached to the center, and a 5- to 10-pound weight attached at the end of the line. The idea is to hold the bar with two outstretched hands and to roll the bar, coiling the line until the weight reaches the bar. Then unwind the line and repeat twice more. This is great for wrists and forearms—key muscle groups for batting and throwing. I had kids use the wrist machine after they batted.

Tell them that you are trying to give them an edge when they come up against their opponents. A kid who does fifty push-ups a day will become very strong. Judge what a player can do and slightly push his limit. Don't ask him to do something that will embarrass him, though. If a player is heavy or out of shape, let him do what he can, and just push it a bit.

I generally recommend that you avoid formal weight training for grade-school kids. They are still growing at a rapid pace. There is a different view, however, and I'll present it in chapter eight.

Don't do wind sprints at the beginning of practice. They require the loosest muscles, so do them at the end of practice. Then do short ones, 60 feet at first (the distance to first base), then 70 feet. Tell the players to reach out in a long stride. Do some sprints backwards and some sideways. Wind sprints are essential for pitchers' leg strength.

Speed Improvement Drills

You can't do much to make a slow kid into a fast one. But you can improve speed significantly, and you can improve running strength, agility, and balance a good deal.

Some drills to improve running speed and form follow. The key is to get kids to run up on the toes and not flat-footed. Teach your players to do the drills early in the season and tell them thereafter to do them on their own. Explain that quickness will help them to get on base or to better run down fly balls.

The Robot. Line up the players and have them run 40 yards at half speed, alternating fist pumps from neck height to just behind the buttocks. The idea is to bang or drive the fists downward in a robotic cadence in rhythm with their stride. Look at track stars in the 100-yard dash and observe how they pump the arms. Have your players run it three times, increasing speed each time.

The Bounce. Similar to the drill above, but players concentrate on lifting their knees high to the chest, bouncing off the ground with each step and lifting the knees as high as possible. Track stars and high jumpers routinely do this drill. It develops the power thrust needed to sprint. After a while, try to incorporate the first drill with the second. Do these for 40 yards.

The Buttkick. Again, run 40 yards and return, this time kicking the heels into the buttocks. This helps the follow-through needed for a complete stride. Every bit of thrust is needed to sprint.

The Goosestep. Finally, run 40 yards in a goosestep, kicking the legs straight out and lifting them straight and high. The idea here is to train to reach out for a greater stride.

Agility Drills

Simon Says. Line up players in several lines of four to five players each. All lines start running in place, in short, quick, choppy steps. The coach signals with his hand for the players to shuffle laterally (without crossing the feet), forward, backward, down to the ground, and up again. Players must square the shoulders, stay low, and react quickly.

Carioca. Line up as above. Players *carioca*, that is, run sideways, left foot over right, then left foot behind right, for 40 yards. Repeat four times.

GOAL TWO: UNDERSTAND EACH PLAYER'S POTENTIAL

You need to figure out what each player can do so he can concentrate on developing the specific skills for his position. You also need to keep an open mind, and, after a while, learn which players you were wrong about. I've seen many coaches quickly decide who plays where and then never change it. Countless times, I've watched a coach stick someone in an odd position late in a meaningless game and suddenly find that the kid is a natural there. While it's important to get things set early so you can concentrate on the special skills required for each position (as discussed in chapter five), you should always be looking to see if someone can help the team somewhere else. Assistant coaches can help you a lot in making these changes and decisions.

A good tool in this respect is to start making lists. Run sprints to see who your fastest players are. Who throws hard? Who can accelerate the fastest (and has short-distance speed)? Who is the most agile? Who are the gutsiest players? Who are the strongest players? Who has the best hands? Once you create these lists, don't throw them away. Check them every couple of weeks to see if someone has earned another look.

The lists force you to evaluate your players according to different aspects of athletic ability. Sometimes you will be surprised to see the name of a player you hadn't been looking at very closely. Constantly evaluate and reevaluate your players. It's incredible to me how rarely some coaches discuss each player. It is far too easy to overlook a quiet kid who may have good ability. Often, something an assistant coach sees will surface in such a full review. Don't label players for the season. Reconsider constantly. Give a kid a shot at something else if he is not working out where you first placed him.

You will find many brief opportunities on the practice field to talk to your players. Ask how is school? How are things at home? What are your interests? You can find out a lot about a kid in just a few minutes. This helps you understand the player, and you will begin to earn his respect, which means he'll work harder to improve for you and for the team.

GOAL THREE: WORK ON INDIVIDUAL AND TEAM SKILLS; USE STATIONS

After ten to fifteen minutes of conditioning, stretching, speed, and agility drills, I like to call the players together. Tell them generally what they will be doing next and what you expect of them. Details can be supplied by assistant coaches. You should focus on individual position skills and fundamentals.

I think it's a great idea to take video or even still pictures of kids at practice. Try to get a parent to volunteer to take some shots of players working on form—batting, pitching, fielding, throwing. Circulate or e-mail the pictures to the kids who need to see what they are doing wrong. Look at stance, arm extension when throwing, how low they are when fielding a grounder. You can meet at someone's house to view the films and talk about form. In coaching, as in art, a picture is truly worth a thousand words.

Working on form and fundamentals is essential. It must start early in the season and continue on a regular basis. If a shortstop's head comes up too soon, if a batter's hands drop, or if the first baseman stretches too soon, let him know. There is no excuse for poor form. A player may not be able to hit every pitch or execute every play well,

115

but he can always employ proper form, and it will help. Have the checklist at the end of the book handy to evaluate form.

I usually divide the team into several groups for batting practice and for defensive practice. The number of small groups, or *stations*, depends on how much help I have. You don't want players daydreaming out in the field during batting practice.

Batting Stations. If you have twelve players and three or more parents (or other assistants) to help out, you can set up three batting stations. Divide the kids into four groups of three players each.

If you have access to a batting net, it will help substantially during batting practice. Perhaps a player owns one and can bring it to practice. They cost anywhere from seventy to a hundred dollars.

Station 1. Take two of the four groups (six kids) to the diamond for regular batting practice. Assign four kids to shag balls, with three in the outfield and one at deep shortstop, or what can be called a short-field position. If parents are available, they can help shag balls, too. Alternate groups of kids between batting and shagging balls.

A parent pitches, preferably down on one knee from 40 feet away. (The parents can rotate pitching.) One kid is at bat and one on deck. Use a bucket of ten to twelve balls. No catcher is needed, and the on-deck player shouldn't pick up balls until all twelve are pitched. After the bucket is empty, the fielders return the retrieved balls; they hold onto them until then. Each batter gets two buckets worth, or about five minutes, whichever is more. Don't waste time, and keep the pitches flowing. If a pitch is errant or the batter misses, quickly throw another ball. If he hits the ball, make sure the fielders are ready, then quickly throw another.

I have my players occasionally take a few pitches batting lefty (or righty if they are lefty). Switch-hitting is more important later on, perhaps by college, when pitches come in a lot faster, because the switch helps a batter see the ball. A lefty batter can see the ball better from a righty pitcher. The ball approaches the plate from more in front of the batter rather than from the side or behind. However, it's good for young kids to switch because it gives them a different perspective. I believe it helps train them to look more closely at the ball, and their swing is less automatic because they have to concentrate more. Have them also hit a couple of bunts.

Station 2. One group of three players goes behind the backstop for the No Pitch Drill. In this drill, the coach or parent lobs the ball from a spot about 6 feet from the plate, off to the side of the batter. Here is where a net about 5 feet away is very handy. The batter faces the net to stop the ball. I once used a clothesline hung between two trees and a heavy blanket to stop the ball. The batter tries to hit the ball dead center, looking at the center spot on the ball. A goal is to hit the ball into the net or screen at waist to chest high—you want line drives. This is a good drill to increase batting practice time without using the field. A variation of this station is to hit off a batting tee. If you don't have a net to hit into, get a bunch of hollow, plastic golf balls and hit them.

Station 3. Three players form this station. They each go through the three steps of the proper swing: stance, loaded stance, and swing. Talk about each step. Work on proper stances. Take some swings. Tell them to visualize the pitch coming in. The coach looks at form and gives instructions. Take forty to fifty swings each. Don't rush the swings.

If you have lots of help to shag balls, then a fourth station can be set up hitting plastic golf balls.

Other batting or running drills listed in chapters two and four, such as Circle Stance, Load-Up, Fifty Strides, Go/Fence, Simon Signs, and Slide Drill and bunting practice, can be separate stations at some point. Rotate the groups of kids in each station every fifteen minutes. If you have three parents, one at each station, you can float around to give pointers where you are most needed. The idea is to use practice time profitably so kids get a lot of repetition and don't get bored. Obviously, if you have little help and only a small playing area, there is only so much you can do. I always tried to figure out some way to keep everyone occupied, and I *always* got parents involved helping out.

Defensive Stations

Break the players into small groups of three or four, depending on the number of coaches, to work on individual skills. If you don't have enough adults, assign a player to be captain of each group if the kids are old enough to take on this responsibility. Do each station for five to ten minutes and then rotate groups among the stations until kids play at each one. Coaches should stay in the same station to gain special expertise.

Station 1. Pepper. This is a fun drill for all players. A coach places three infielders side by side about 10 feet or less from him. The coach hits grounders to them with a bat, and the infielders throw the ball back low, directly to the bat for another grounder. This improves reflexes. (See figure 7-2 on page 118.)

7-2. PEPPER

Line up several infielders. Tap out grounders. Have player toss ball back directly to the bat for next tap.

Station 2. Infield Fungo Drill. This is the bread-and-butter practice for infielders. A coach or parent hits grounders from the plate to infielders in three positions—at first, shortstop, and third. He also hits shallow pop-ups to the infield. Infielders practice throwing to the first baseman who then rolls the ball home. A nice variation of this drill is the Machine Gun Drill. Stand midway between the plate and the pitcher's mound, and fire grounders at one fielder. As soon as the fielder releases the throw back to the catcher, fire another at the same player. Speed it up as fast as that player can handle it, then go on to another player.

Station 3. Outfield Fungo Drill. This is a basic drill for outfielders. The coach lines up in foul territory along third base and hits pop-ups, line drives, and hard grounders. It might work better to throw the pop-ups (if your arm can take it). Have one player in close to relay the ball. At young ages, use a softer ball.

Station 4. Outtahere Drill. Place a loose bag in the outfield away from any other station, near a long strip of cardboard. The fielders line up and take turns straddling the bag, preparing to tag a runner out. Have a coach throw to the fielder as runners slide into the tag. Have a player stand on the edge of the cardboard so it doesn't slide. Tell the kids to slide into the bag and avoid their teammate's feet.

Other drills mentioned in chapter three can be used as stations also, such as Rapid Fire, Goalie Grounder, Bat Drill, and Target Practice.

Specialty Stations

Specialty stations begin to focus on certain positions. Except for station two on stances and station eight for pitchers, I usually don't use these at first, but work them in after a few weeks.

Station 1. Lob Drill. With three players in position, hit a grounder to the first baseman. He lobs the ball to the pitcher, who runs to cover first. The third player runs to first, but does not step on the bag, just runs past it. Be sure players know not to collide. A variation is to hit grounders between short and second, hitting close to the bag (10 feet is fine) so that players can lob to each other.

Station 2. Stance Station. With a group of three or four players, go over the fundamentals of the defensive stances of their positions. If a kid is a catcher, talk about the catcher's crouch. The tuck of a catcher is reminiscent of a downhill skier. If he is a first baseman, talk about the first baseman's stance and stretch. Go over form for fielding grounders and outfield flies. Focus on the player's specialty, and also review form for other positions he may play. Have the players demonstrate the form. Look at each aspect: feet, torso, both hands, balance, and position near the batter. Use the checklist in chapter ten to make sure you don't forget anything.

Station 3. Wild Thing Drill. The catcher is in full gear behind the plate. The first baseman alternates with the catcher (he should also wear a mask and shin guard). The coach throws the ball, alternating players, and throws it high, low into the dirt, inside, and out. The idea is to get the catcher and first baseman to practice handling wild throws and throws in the dirt. They will see plenty of these throws during a game and need to be able to stop them. A player or parent can throw the errant balls; make sure the pitcher can place the ball at difficult but still catchable spots. Don't make it too hard at first.

Station 4. Pop-Up Drill. Great for catchers, pitchers, and infielders. The coach stands at the plate (this station can be set up anywhere) and lobs the ball with backspin, straight up in the air. The catcher should spring from the crouch to locate and catch the ball. Other fielders also come in for the ball.

Station 5. Get Bunt Drill. The ball is bunted down the first baseline. The catcher scrambles from a crouch, and the pitcher charges in to scoop it up (two hands) and throw to first. First one there calls it. If it's a tie, the pitcher should yield to the catcher. Step to the infield side of the line to ensure the ball doesn't hit the runner.

Station 6. Passed Ball Drill. Most steals are on passed balls (balls missed by the catcher). The catcher should practice hustling to the ball, snatching it up and preparing to throw. Have a kid on first base run to second as the ball hits the backstop. Work the catcher on the optimum time to throw and when not to throw. It's important for the catcher to know when he has a chance to get the runner out and, just as important, to know when there is no chance and a throw only risks another error. The catcher has only a split second to decide as he glimpses the runner's position; it is a situation that must be practiced. Even more important is the drill when a runner is on third. See chapter five for details on getting the ball to the pitcher covering the plate.

Station 7. Rundown Drills. All infielders, pitchers, and catchers should do this drill. Use different groups for different bases. Remember, each baseman must be backed up. (See chapter three for more information on which players cover each base.)

    i. **Catcher, pitcher, third base, shortstop.** Rundown between third and home. Instruct the first and second basemen to cover their bags. Left fielder backs up third.

    ii. **Pitcher, third base, shortstop, second base.** Rundown between third base and second base. Catcher and first baseman cover their bases.

    iii. **Shortstop, second base, first base, pitcher.** Rundown between second base and first base. Catcher and third baseman cover their bases.

Station 8. Pitchers. The key to pitching is proper form. Study the form fundamentals in chapter five. Get the pitchers in a group at each practice. You can do it off to the side for what I call a Sideline Pitch Drill. Have the catcher or a parent catch. Use something for a pitcher's rubber and something for a home plate. Don't try to change too much at once; one thing at a time is best. Have the pitcher look at pictures of the six parts of proper pitching form: address, rocker, crane, kick, drive and "open the door," and follow-through. Talk about grip and opening the hips.

Have them learn control by the hitting the corners: high and outside, high and tight, low and inside, and low and away. Go around the four corners three or four times, then take a break and do it again. Practice pitching from a stretch and holding a runner (by looking back toward second base).

Team Execution Stations

The last half hour of practice, get the team together for drills that require a full set of fielders and base runners. For these drills, players should be in their regular positions.

Station 1. Cutoff Drills. Start with the bases empty, then add runners to first, then first and second, then load the bases. Hit the ball to any fielder, infield or out. Get the kids into the habit of thinking ahead to where they will go with the ball. Talk about their choices and execution after each play. Run through each cutoff play for each outfielder, but pepper a few grounders at infielders to keep them on their toes. If the ball gets through, then make sure they make the cutoff play. Play live conditions: rundowns, slides (if the field is not too rough), and tagouts.

Station 2. Partial Scrimmage. There is usually not enough time to play a game, but if you organize the practice well, you can sometimes get a few innings in. I divide up the kids and parents. Parents play the outfield. Usually, I just use parents as steady defense, but some want to take a few swings, too. I do the pitching to make sure the ball is hittable. It also saves the pitchers' arms.

Station 3. Signals. The Stay or Go Drill is designed to work runners with the third base coach. Line up the team midway between second and third base and let them come in one at a time. Give one of four signs to stay, slide, turn the corner, or go home (see chapter four). Another good drill is Simon Signs (see page 67). Gather the team around you and review the signs. Give them a key sign and go through a series of signs. The first one to get the sign yells it out.

THE PRACTICE PLAN

Each practice should have a written practice plan. It takes just a few minutes to think through what you want to accomplish, and it does wonders for efficient use of time. You can waste a lot of practice time if you are not organized, and you can triple the value of the practice if you are.

Practice plans vary over the course of a season. The focus of the first weeks of practice, usually starting in April for grade-school-level play, is (1) batting and defensive practice; (2) figuring out what positions each player can play; and (3) conditioning. Focus then shifts to individual skills and to team dynamics. Note that I said the focus changes—however, all of these concepts are involved in every week's practice throughout the year.

The following are typical sample practice plans for different weeks in the season. I start at 5:30 P.M. on weekdays, since coaches at grade-school levels have day jobs. In April it may stay light until 7:30 P.M. A Saturday practice usually lasts two and a half hours.

Early April: Tuesday Practice Plan

Early birds run a lap and have a catch to warm up the arm.

5:30 P.M. Conditioning: Have players do Quick Cali Set drills; several from the Leg Stretch Set; also select one drill from Speed Drills (Robot, Bounce, Buttkick, Goosestep) and one from Agility Drills Set (Simon Says, Carioca).

5:50 P.M. Call team together. Brief comments.

6:00 P.M. Batting Stations. Do batting station one and select two to three other batting and running drills for about fifteen minutes.

6:30 P.M. Five-Minute Water Break: Continue batting stations.

7:10 P.M. Defensive Stations. Do three stations, five to six minutes each. Evaluate defensive potential of each player. On grounders, infielders should make the throw to first base. However, avoid too much throwing, and after a while, have them just field the ball and lob it home.

7:10 P.M. Pitchers Station. Simultaneous with defensive work, do the Sideline Pitch Drill with a coach or other pitchers catching. Use four pitchers at a time. Go five minutes, with two pitching and the other two catching, then switch. Then bring in four more. Find out who can pitch.

7:25 P.M. Wind Sprints.

7:30 P.M. Closing Comments, Practice Over.

Late April: Saturday Practice Plan

Early birds run a lap and have a catch to warm up the arm.

9:30 A.M. Conditioning: Quick Cali Set, Leg Stretch Set.

9:40 A.M. Call team together. Brief comments.

9:50 A.M. Batting Stations. Do three to four stations for eight to nine minutes each.

10:20 A.M. Five-Minute Water Break: Continue batting stations.

10:50 A.M. Defensive Stations: Do three stations. Five minutes each.

11:05 A.M. Specialty Drills: Set up three stations, only one of which requires the batter's box. Six to seven minutes each.

11:25 P.M. Wind Sprints.

11:30 P.M. Closing Comments, Practice Over.

May Practice: A Weekday

Early birds run a lap and have a catch to warm up the arm.

5:30 P.M. Conditioning: Do a Quick Cali Set, Leg Stretch Set.

5:40 P.M. Call team together. Brief comments.

5:45 P.M. Batting Stations. Do three to four stations for eight to nine minutes each.

6:20 P.M. Five-Minute Water Break. Continue batting stations.

6:45 P.M. Specialty Stations. Set up three, five minutes each.

7:00 P.M. Team Execution Stations. Choose one.

7:25 P.M. Wind Sprints.

7:30 P.M. Closing Comments, Practice Over.

These plans work well for most age groups. At younger ages, you can shorten the conditioning a bit and spend more time talking baseball. Get the kids in a circle and ask them questions: What's a steal? What's a ball? What's a strike? Who can name the fielding positions? What's a triple, a homer, a double, a single?

Get them all around home plate and demonstrate proper stance and swing form. Tell them about bad form. Demonstrate defensive form. Spend a fair amount of time each practice until they have it right. For younger kids, it will take longer and be less productive to spend time in specialty drills, but make sure you acquaint the players with every concept and do a few drills. Of course, they need a lot of time batting and fielding.

07

08 ON COACHING AND WINNING

I define coaching as the art of inspiring a child to understand that they can draw something greater from themselves in their efforts to succeed. That's the mission, and all else flows from that purpose. It's all about the kids and helping them to become better—better athletes and better people.

HOW DO YOU WANT TO BE REMEMBERED?

Throughout his baseball experience, a kid finds out about himself—for good or bad—and he will always associate his feelings with you. Coaching is an awesome responsibility. The relationship between a coach and a player is a powerful one. You are not only a parental figure, but you are the final authority in what is, in his mind, perhaps the most important thing in life.

You may want to ignore this larger picture, but it will not change what's really going on. Most of your players will never make the cut at the high-school level, a few may play in college, and you will likely never coach a future pro baseball player. However, every one of your players will become an adult someday, with the responsibility of a job and probably a family as well. It is doubtful that they will remember much about this season twenty years from now, certainly not the scores of various games. But I guarantee you one thing: They will remember you for the rest of their lives. The memories of my coaches are etched clearly in my mind. I remember them vividly, for good or for bad. You may not remember all of the kids you coached, particularly if you do it for a number of years, but every one of them will remember you. How do you want to be remembered?

This book provides many tools you can use to help make the experience a good one, regardless of whether you win or lose as a team.

ON WINNING

08

Feelings on the importance of winning run strong. As with religion and politics, everyone thinks they are right. Vince Lombardi, the legendary Green Bay Packer football coach, once said, "Winning isn't everything ... it's the only thing." Many will say if you are going to keep a score, you should try to win.

Let's face it: If you tell kids that winning is no big deal, they may nod, but they are not really buying it. They *know* about winning. They know the kids on the other team will gloat and taunt them back at school. They know about trophies and news articles. They hear the empty silence after a loss.

Well, the truth of it is somewhere in the middle. Kids talk about winning, but I believe that down deep they care even more about how well they are personally doing. I remember one year in my playing days when I was in a terrible slump. The team was winning, but was that satisfactory to me? No way! I was playing lousy. Another year, we lost a championship game, but I hit a home run. How did I feel? You guessed it. Sure I wanted to win, but the homer went a long way toward easing the pain.

All right, winning is important in the pros. And maybe it's important for some players in high school, where scholarship money rarely goes to anyone on a team with a 3-26 record. But in Little League, it's just not important. Parents and coaches may think it is, but the kids often forget the game—and certainly the score—as soon as they hit the nearest pool. What they will remember is how they felt about themselves and how you treated them.

PRACTICAL ADVICE

I tell my kids something they can believe—that winning is never important in Little League, but that it is always fun. That's the truth. They can relate to it. I tell them that what's important is how they handle victory or defeat. It's important to help each other and to try to play their best. We surely try to win, but all we can really control is how hard we try.

Competition stirs up some powerful emotions. It's said that winning builds character, while losing reveals it. Competitive fire can quickly melt an otherwise cool, calm, collected attitude. At the heart of how good a coach you are is how well you balance your need to win with the need to develop healthy young people. The balance will affect your every action, your relationship with each player, and the atmosphere on the field; it will characterize the memories of your coaching experience for many years to come. Striking that balance involves a continual struggle between the passions fired up by competition on the one hand, and the caring you feel for your players as a responsible adult on the other.

I find that balance in light of how much talent I have on a team. When I see that we have little chance of winning it all, I choose to emphasize individual goals. Let's face it: If you can't get there, there is absolutely no sense in getting everyone crazy. But when you have a potential championship team . . . that's the real test!

The key is balance. Winning and development both are part of the game. For instance, we all worry about the total dedication required of young Olympic athletes who have sacrificed much of their youth for their quests. Yet we know they have enjoyed moments of glory that seem to transcend life itself, achieving heights most of us only dream about.

ON COMPETITION

"Our society is ferociously competitive in spirit. Pressuring children too hard may turn them into adults so obsessed with being first that they get no joy out of life except in the narrow field of competition. They neither give nor get pleasure in their relationships with spouses, children, friends, and fellow workers."

—*Dr. Benjamin Spock*

This warning makes a lot of sense and strongly urges us to be more vigilant against over-stressing winning. Yet, we also need to understand that competition has a rightful and perhaps intractable place in our society. If this is true, then shouldn't we prepare our children to deal with it?

It's just not realistic when "experts" like Alfie Kohn tell us in the book *No Contest: The Case Against Competition* that analysis of years of psychological research proves that "competition is poison." That is like telling us not to breathe because the air is somewhat polluted. Competition is a part of life, period. We all know kids who could have excelled, but did not do so. They just needed a good push or some self-confidence to get going.

Obviously, competition can be taken to extremes. Many years ago there was n ugly scene on national television when competitive fire drove Ohio State coaching legend Woody Hayes to assault an opposing Clemson player on the field. And we cringed when young tennis star Mary Pierce, symbolic of many troubled young athletes, had to obtain a restraining order against her father for pressuring her. The frenzy to win, riding on the dark horse of fear of failure, can and does get both crazy and destructive.

The issue of competition goes to the essence of the human condition. It is part of our evolution. The answers are complex and most elusive.

I recently read in *The New York Times* that some schools are abandoning competitive interaction in their physical education programs to avoid damaging the feelings of kids who are not outstanding. Isn't it better for kids to learn about and prepare for success and failure in a controlled setting, inside the relatively harmless gymnasium, rather than in the crucible of adult life? Should we abandon youth competition just because we, as a society, haven't figured out how to always do it right? We couldn't quit if we wanted to. It's part of life and we must continue to work to find the best balance.

Winning and growth do share common ground. Coaches who win consistently are remembered by their former players more for their great lessons of life than for the gold cup on the mantel. Great coaches know that the key to success is to motivate athletes to win the personal struggles, to do their best, to improve beyond their limits, spurred on by their team's goals. They know that the spirit, the will to win, and the will to excel transcend the game itself. Even kids who will never play beyond youth baseball or win big championships can still excel, improve, and gain personal satisfaction from making a putout or getting on base.

How you resolve the balance between winning and individual development is up to you. If you just recognize the need to strike a balance, you are off to a good start.

My own approach in coaching is probably best characterized by a back-and-forth struggle around that balance. When I find myself too focused on the win, I step back. I remind myself that while we're going for it, we need to stay on the high road. Every coach has felt that gut-wrenching feeling that stays with him for hours after a game. It's enough to be honest about the reality of competitive passion, and then to commit ourselves as coaches to doing what we expect of our players, and doing our best with it. I believe most coaches want to build character and a positive experience for each player while trying to win the game.

Some coaches never really challenge their teams for fear of upsetting the kids, and these "nice guys" don't do much damage. Of course, their players may never make it to the next level of play. Other coaches, at the opposite extreme, feel compelled to win at all costs, and the cost can be tragic for the fragile psyche of a young child. Find the middle ground. If you find you can't deal with the pressure, consider whether coaching is right for you and for the kids.

The practical way to get a reality check is to pick out a parent who seems be open and who knows the other parents well and ask how things are going. Parents talk to each other about how they feel and how their kids are feeling, and you can learn things that they might not tell you directly.

Of course, the issues vary with the age of your team. At preteen levels, the emphasis is always heavily on developing the individual. This doesn't mean that winning is not an issue; it's just not all-important. The focus is solely on development. This is why most programs require that all kids play a certain amount of time. By high-school varsity play, the balance is more even. It should never get further than that, but the reality of major collegiate play is that losing coaches don't last.

ON MOTIVATION

Some coaches have a charismatic quality and can motivate a team just by the sheer strength of their personalities. However, most of us mere "mortal" coaches need to consider motivational techniques to help us get the job done.

The "secrets" to good motivation are easily found in the growing science of sports psychology. Once considered mere gobbledygook, the mental aspect of competition is now a cornerstone of athletic development at the highest levels of amateur and professional sports. Many teams, including the U.S. Olympic program, employ full-time sports psychologists.

It is not the purpose of this book to go into the psychology of sports. You will find aspects of psychology spread throughout, as well as in my books on coaching other youth sports such as basketball, football, and soccer. I have used psychological insight throughout my thirty years of coaching, and much of it is common sense and obvious to any caring adult. The first chapters of this book focused on confidence-building and on the right mental approach to the game. My checklist approach to teaching correct form is consistent with the mental checklist urged for athletes by sports psychologists.

If you want to focus more deeply in this area, one of the best books I've read on the subject is *The Athlete's Guide to Sports Psychology: Mental Skills for Physical People*, by Dorothy V. Harris and Bette L. Harris. I will, however, discuss some emerging motivational techniques that seem to work best.

ATTABOY!

There will never be a better tool than frequent positive reinforcement for young athletes. This is especially true for baseball where there are many more strikes and outs than hits for a young athlete. It is essential to liberally give out some attaboys for good effort. In *Kidsports: A Survival Guide for Parents*, Dr. Nathan J. Smith, a consultant for the American Board of Pediatrics, reported on his study of two groups of coaches. He found that "the single most important difference in our research between coaches

128

to whom young athletes respond most favorably and those to whom they respond least favorably was the frequency with which coaches reinforce and reward desirable behavior." A pat on the back, a smile, clapping, praise, a wink and a nod, as well as tangible rewards such as a mention in a newspaper article or more playing time, all go a very long way toward motivating high performance. I would add that the rewards are even more effective when they emphasize outstanding effort as opposed to great results. An athlete has complete control over the amount of effort he puts into his game, but the results depends on many things, most of which are beyond the individual's control. Even corrective action or pointing out mistakes should be sandwiched within some positive comments, such as "Good try, Jack. Next time, keep your eye on the ball. You can do it!"

Coaches spend a lot of time hollering, trying to motivate players, trying to get them to increase their energy levels, and trying to develop that all-important desire to perform. However, there is a line that shouldn't be crossed. You should *never* humiliate a player. Be firm and let the player know that he can do better if he reaches deeper into his gut. I like to ask players if they gave it their best shot. "Was that your best effort?" "Do you have more 'pop' in your bat?"

Having one set of standards for everyone doesn't mean you shouldn't handle players differently. Some kids respond well when you correct them in front of their peers. Others are devastated when you get on them, even if done calmly. You will quickly get a feel from their reaction to you. Take these kids aside and explain what you saw. Some kids will seem troubled all the time, so sit down with them and find out what's going on in their lives; see if you can learn what the problem is.

At advanced levels, your expectations for performance are much higher. Players will generally have the skills, and it is the lapses in concentration that most affect performance. The focus of the criticism here may be a firm, "Make sure you are focused!" but in a controlled tone. Yelling will get a kid's attention, but it will also humiliate him. There is a way to get his attention and still be positive. As noted earlier, the essence of coaching is to inspire an athlete to be all he can be, and coaching criticism must be grounded in the notion that the player can do better.

Let a player know what you think about his effort, not himself. Don't personalize it. The kid is a decent person: It's the effort you want more of, so focus on the effort during practice. A kid can relate to trying harder; but he can't relate positively to your telling him he stinks. Explain the problem with fundamentals or form so that he understands the concept. Work with him until he gets the idea.

Most importantly, reward good effort openly and liberally. Praise a good catch. Recognize hustle. Yell out, "That's baseball!" A positive attitude can be infectious, with all players trying to listen for and praise the sound of good bat contact.

MOTIVATIONAL PHRASES

HITTING

Ya gotta believe.
You're a hitter.
Swing a hard bat.
Swing with confidence.
Smack a good pitch.
You can hit this guy.

AFTER A BAD AT BAT

Learn from it.
Shake it off, get the next one.
We'll get it back.
Get a better pitch.
Good cut, see the ball better.
Your turn next time.

FIELDING

Run it down.
Get under it.
Nothing past you.
Want the ball.

AFTER A LOSS

Good effort. Was it your best?
How much do you want it?

We got to swing more.

We need to run smarter.

We're better than this.

Let's focus more next time.

AFTER A WIN

It was a team win.

Super effort.

It's happening.

That's baseball.

You earned it.

Don't gloat, just smile.

FUGGEDDABOUTIT!!!

Kids need to know that they will lose sometimes, and so it's useful to talk about it and point out that at youth levels, the only important thing is learning. The key is to understand that losing and learning are the same things; losing is just another learning experience. The only important thing is to do your best and get better. When the loss occurs, remind them of these things: Winning is fun, but learning is all that matters now!

WE ARE FAMILY!

I've read the autobiographies of many great coaches. One constant in all of their stories is the ability to relate to the different individuals on their teams and to create a family-type environment.

Each kid is different, whether on a team or in a family, and each one needs a personal approach. Even the last substitute should be treated with respect equal to that of the best players. I start each season with a team discussion on what it means to be on a team. I tell the players that for the rest of the season, they are all friends. They are all in a special relationship with each other. I tell them they should say hello in the school hallways, and help each other out, off the field, if needed. I never tolerate criticism of a teammate on the field and quickly bench any offender. I expect kids to urge each other on, and to quickly tell a teammate to put a mistake behind him. I promote team dinners and outings, and I move to break up cliques.

131

Team building is a proven ticket to success. The concept is widely used in all walks of life and is a staple of business organization. Team building doesn't just happen because a bunch of kids are on a team. It happens because coaches work at it. It's actually quite easy to get done. Just put it in the practice plan, talk to your assistant coaches about it, and opportunities to promote team unity will present themselves in abundance.

SET GOALS

To give kids proper motivation, you must set realistic goals for the team and for each individual. With specific goals, a kid has something clear and achievable to work on, something to set his sights on. He is not responsible for the whole team or for winning or losing. He is not overwhelmed and defeated by unrealistic expectations. Goals provide stimulation.

I think it's a good idea to have each player set his own goals under guidance of the coach. I usually offer the players a number of categories in which a few goals should be set. One category is conditioning. The goals may be to double the number of push-ups they can do, or to knock some time off their wind sprints. Other goals relate to specific skills for their positions. It may be to improve the form of the swing or of the fielding position. Still other goals relate to game performance, such as number of hits. I might also suggest to a player that he increase his self-confidence, his self-control, his relationship with certain teammates, or his effort at practice. I'll have the player write it down, and we'll occasionally review progress. Don't set too many goals; just focus on key areas.

DON'T UNDERESTIMATE YOUR KIDS

Aren't kids too young to learn all of these baseball skills? Well, if your players are very young, it will be a while before they understand the more complex skills and routinely do them well on the field. But all concepts, including the more complicated strategies of throwing ahead of the lead runner and the cutoff, should be taught, or at least started, at all age levels. Don't underestimate your players; some of them will grasp these concepts. The basics, especially hitting form and fielding stances, should be emphasized right away before bad habits form. I pitched to my kids as soon as they could hold bats, and I insisted they employ proper form.

A lot of refinements, such as using the cutoff, backing up positions, and the rundown technique, take time and maturity. I had a group of ten-year-old All-Stars one year, and I drilled them on more advanced cutoff concepts. I knew they would not actually use most of it for a long time, but they had never even been exposed to it and had to start sometime. If parents and coaches set the stage in early years, some of the advanced concepts will click by age ten. But if your players are green, don't worry about it. Concentrate on the basics, and go over the advanced stuff, but don't expect too much too soon.

Believe me when I say there is no magic age for starting baseball. Look at the kids mastering moves in gymnastics, soccer, and other sports at seven and eight years old. It's not that younger kids can't learn. They just need someone who understands complex concepts and has the time and ability to teach them. A lot depends on how much time you have to practice; unfortunately, weather and field availability are usually problems.

There isn't anything in this book that's over the heads of young kids. Just start somewhere, and the kids will absorb as much as you have the time and patience to teach them. Some skills will take a few sessions, some require much more, some will take years, but it will happen. Like learning how to whistle, one day it's suddenly there, and you sense it was always really simple to do.

ON PEAK PERFORMANCE

The bane of coaches is whatever makes a kid play great one day and completely fall apart the next day. A kid gets struck out his first time up and winds up walking around in a daze all day. Another kid makes a good catch and suddenly starts to terrorize the batter's box. One day the shortstop can't find the first baseman even if they were holding hands; other days his play seems transcendent.

Modern science tells us that how we cope with the stress of a challenge is largely mental; it's all upstairs. There's not a kid alive who hasn't felt those butterflies in the stomach. Under game conditions, this reaction can create a feeling of panic that interrupts concentration and even causes muscle spasms. However, when controlled properly, it can lead the athlete to a "zone" of peak performance.

In its February 14, 1994, issue, *U.S. News and World Report*, in an article entitled "The Inner Game of Winning," reported on the research of Stanford University neurobiologist Robert Sapolsky. He found that a properly controlled response to challenge releases a desirable increase in adrenaline and sugar, producing the sense of *zone*. The negative counterpart of this reaction, which he calls the *fearful response*, produces a bodily cocktail laced with a substance called cortisol that can "not only impair performance, but can also lead over the long run to damage of the arteries and liver, and lead to depression."

STEPS TO IMPROVE PEAK PERFORMANCE

The research suggests several steps coaches can take to create or strive for the conditions optimal to peak performance.

Coaches have been doing some of this for years. The time-honored way to produce a controlled response to game-day excitement is constant repetition during practice. This book suggests repeatedly practicing hitting and fielding, including adherence to proper form. Game responses should become automatic and will occur even if the player is under stress or too excited.

The studies also suggest that a ritual-like approach to game day is conducive to a relaxed state of mind. A regular pattern of eating, exercise, dressing, and pregame discussion is highly recommended. Try to avoid any surprises or deviations. The preset mental routine should apply right up to each pitch during the game.

Sports psychologists have long supported mental imaging of athletic routines. Olympic athletes have been tracing their steps mentally for years. What we have now are clear scientific bases for these approaches. These techniques are useful at all levels of play. They are perhaps most needed at the youngest levels, where kids cannot control the anxieties of competition.

Sapolsky notes that premature arousal of adrenalin hours before the game can result in a drop in the level in the blood after a few hours, to a point below normal at game time. This will lead to subpar performance and is another reason to have relaxed, stable pregame routines. Many coaches now employ Zen-type meditations in their training programs, providing athletes with methods to evoke relaxed states of mind at will.

A lot of coaches have a concept they use to focus players on achieving peak performance. I always told my players to try to get an edge over their opponents. We talked about how evenly matched most good teams usually are, and that the winner would be the team who got some kind of edge over their opponents.

This concept helped me to get kids to accept, for instance, the idea of improving mental approach as one way to get an edge. I would also tell kids to double the number of push-ups they could do, since kids on the other teams probably weren't doing so, and they could get a bit stronger and gain an advantage over them.

ON PARENTS

As you know, parents can be a great help in youth sports; however, interfering parents can be a major problem for coaches. This is especially true in baseball because parents are usually right on top of the team, and their complaining is more visible. Note that more modern youth baseball complexes have placed the bleachers beyond the outfield fences. I find this is too far away to see my grandchildren hit, but I understand the purpose.

I have no problem with parents who, after the game, want to talk to the coach and find out whether there is a problem they need to be aware of. But often they are argumentative, and sometimes they are downright insulting. Of course, you don't need to take abuse from any parent. Before you get too defensive, think about what's going on.

Most parents literally die a little bit when they see their children going through a bad time. Maybe the kid is not playing much, having self-doubts, and acting out at home or at school because of it. A parent feels the pain along with the kid—it's tough for a kid, or anyone, to feel he's not good enough. So, hear the parent out. Gain an understanding of the problem and perhaps focus on things the parent can do to help the child. Tell the parent that you think the child can do better and you are trying to arouse his potential. Maybe you can get some insight into what is troubling the child. Maybe, just maybe, you are dead wrong, and you need to give the kid another look. Tell parents you will consider what they have said. I've seen kids who sat on the bench as a sub for half a season suddenly come alive and wind up starting the rest of the season.

Most of all, keep in mind that you're talking about their kids! Parents may feel a bit threatened by your control over their child. As a parent, I have had uneasy feelings about coaches—it's quite natural. A little patience on your part can defuse some strong emotions. You can turn a potential feud into something that helps the child, and ultimately the team. Try it.

On the other hand, parents who abuse their children during a game are a major problem. These are the parents who scorn their children for striking out or missing a catch. It's the worst thing in sports to see. You do not have to put up with this! Talk to such parents and ask them to keep quiet. If they don't, remove them from the field.

One parent threatened me with removing his son as well. My response was merely that I hoped he wouldn't, but that not playing was better than what was going on, and that it would not continue under my watch. The parent stayed home; the kid played.

Frankly, as noted earlier, I rarely have problems with parents. When you can achieve a certain level of team spirit, it becomes infectious, and negativity gets left behind. I always seek to empower parents and to get them involved with the team in some manner: as coaches or ball-shaggers; providing water breaks; running fund drives; managing uniforms; or organizing phone trees. Delegate as much as possible, and you'll bring parents into the team dynamic. Chapter seven on planning practices pointed to ways that

135

parents can keep more activities going during practices. Parents who are athletes can pitch batting practice, hit fungoes, even instruct specialty drills. Encourage parents to bring a glove and have a catch with their children before practice to warm up players' arms. A parent stationed in the outfield can help keep players focused. Parents in foul territory can retrieve balls. Push gently to get them involved, but don't push too hard.

NOTES FOR PARENTS

HOW CAN I GET MY CHILD INTERESTED IN BASEBALL?

The most important way is to avoid the negative stuff. If your child is afraid of the ball, fearful of being embarrassed, or tired of your impatience (if you are yelling at him and getting annoyed or frustrated), he will never be interested. Tell him he is a hitter already, and you are going to work with him to develop batting skills. Communicate. Discuss the things in this book. Talk baseball, or go to a pro game or to a local high-school game. Watch some baseball on television. Work with your child to collect a whole series of baseball cards. If you go out and coach him and he gets better, you won't have to worry about his interest level.

I coached my three children in many sports, and often I got home from work and found one of them waiting for me, perhaps with a ball and two gloves. "Hey, Dad, want to catch a few?" Interest? I couldn't turn it off. If you work closely with your child on something like this, he will not only be interested in baseball, he'll become interested in you, and you in him. How can you lose?

BEHAVIOR AT GAMES

I'm not going to tell you to just sit there and be quiet. I'm not going to tell you to reduce your energy by one iota. But if you read this book carefully, you know what to do at games. First, don't add any pressure to your child or anyone's child. Second, say intelligent, helpful things like, "Keep your eye on the ball," "Keep the elbow up," "On your toes," "Two outs," "You're a hitter," things that will help your child to remember the basics. See the sidebar "Motivational Phrases" for good phrases to call out. If your son swings and misses, yell, "Good cut!" Yell, "Get a better pitch next time." Be positive.

If a batter strikes out swinging, I always clap my hands. A batter who swings will hit the ball at some point. I want the batter who strikes out swinging to feel good about having swung. On the other hand, if a batter takes a called third strike and the ball was over the plate, I don't yell anything. I take the player to the side and we talk about the fact that you can't have fun unless you swing the bat.

136

Another thing you can do at games is get to know the other parents on your team. It's really a beautiful thing when teams become one big family. Most of mine have been that way because I make it a high priority. It makes everything looser, more relaxed, and it's better for the kids. It also can lead to some rewarding friendships and to a deeper feeling of community, and that's icing on the cake. In addition, you might get another parent more interested in helping his child, and that's super. Finally, tell other parents to read this book.

HOW TO DEAL WITH THE COACH

I hope you will have read this book and practiced with your child for a few years before you ever meet your child's first coach. Then you can offer your help as an assistant or even sign up for the top job. When kids are six to eight years old, there is not much skill on the field to worry about. It is a good starting place for inexperienced coaches.

If you don't coach, I suggest you find another way to get involved. When the coach calls, offer whatever help you can give. If your job prohibits weekdays, offer to help on weekends. Many coaches will be happy for it. (If you run into a coach who doesn't want help, there's not much you can do, but you can still work with your child at home.)

Just walk up to the coach at practice and ask if you can help. Suggest taking a few kids off to the side to have a catch. You can back up the batters for foul pops or help with outfield practice. You can supply some water for breaks. Offer to help with phone calls. Some parents just like to sit and watch practice. I don't mind, and most coaches won't either. Besides, it will help you become aware of areas where your child can use some improvement.

If the coach is a negative person, and you will probably get one for your child at some point, you should let the Little League board know about it. Bad coaches need to be weeded out. They can do a lot of damage.

If your child is playing the minimum, but only the minimum, be fair before you approach the coach. Usually, coaches are out to win, and they do play the best players. Work a little harder with your child at home, and he may improve enough to play more. If the coach is being unfair, talk to him about it. It is difficult for all involved, so please be sure it's not just your ego complaining. And, for goodness sake, keep your child out of the debate. Kids don't need the negative images involved. Don't get mad, since the coach may take it out on your child, but don't duck it either. A few questions to the coach, nicely stated, will help.

09

CONDITIONING

I rarely recommend weight training for youth sports, and I certainly don't recommend it for baseball. I'll discuss this later in this section. A good calisthenics program is adequate, and a list of exercises can be found in chapter seven. Push-ups are the best baseball exercise for upper-body strength. Tell your players to try to build up to thirty to forty per day (if under ten years old, ten to twenty reps is okay). Chin-ups, as many as the player can do, are also quite helpful. Wrist, forearm, and shoulder strength are crucial, and any work you do here will be immediately and quite noticeably rewarded on the field. I got my son a set of chest expanders, with springs attached to handles, and he used them while watching cartoons. The wrist machine mentioned in chapter seven is great for home or practice. I always had one in my duffel bag, and the kids used it after they batted. Rowing exercises are also very good to increase strength and stamina. Pitchers especially need forearm and wrist strength to snap the ball.

After the chest come the legs. Wind sprints are the best leg exercise. Partial squats, halfway bending the knee with some extra weight added, are quite good. Kids shouldn't bend all the way. The long-standing tradition of running up stairs is excellent. If you have a weight bench, the leg extender apparatus is also very good.

Whenever using weights, focus only on strength conditioning. Use low weight with multiple repetitions. High weight just pumps up size, and that is not needed, particularly at youth-level play.

Muscles are like bubble gum. If you stretch gum quickly, it tears or snaps, but if you stretch it slowly, it expands nicely. Stretching before practice and games will help prevent muscles from tearing or snapping. No practice of any kind should begin without slow jogging, some jumping jacks (for the ankles), and general stretching (for the upper thigh, trunk, and neck). Running sideways and backwards or any agility exercises are quite good also.

138

As noted, I generally believe that weight training should be avoided by grade-school-level players and not started until mid-high-school years. Part of the reason is intuitive: A child's body is growing rapidly until then. Some studies done in the 1970s have demonstrated that grade-school kids do not gain strength from weight lifting due to lack of male hormones. These studies also suggested that there was significant risk of injury to kids' growth plates, which are the ends of the long bones that account for growth.

A careful study of 354 high-school football players by Dr. William Risser of the University of Texas Medical School found that weight lifting can cause severe musculoskeletal injuries, usually muscle strains and often in the lower back—7.1 percent of the players reported injury. Injuries occurred when free weights were used in major lifts such as the clean and jerk, the snatch, the squat lift, the dead lift, the power clean, and in the bench, incline, and overhead presses. Most injuries occurred in the home and were related to poor technique and form, lack of warm-up, and lack of a spotter to assist.

However, I must report that more recent research suggests a different point of view from my own. In the November 1990 issue of *Pediatrics* (Vol. 86, No. 5), the American Academy of Pediatrics Committee on Sports Medicine said, "Recent research has shown that short-term programs in which prepubescent [grade school] athletes are trained and supervised by knowledgeable adults can increase strength without significant injury risk. Strength training in adolescence occasionally produces significant musculoskeletal injury … especially during use of the major lifts. Safety requires careful planning of several aspects of a program. This includes devising a program for the intensity, duration, frequency, and rate of progression of weight use, as well as selection of sport-specific exercises appropriate for the physical maturity of the individual. Proper supervision should be provided during training sessions."

The committee also addressed the issue of when kids should be allowed to lift maximal amounts of weight, that is, the heaviest amount of weight they can successfully lift. They concluded that it should be avoided until kids have passed the period of maximal velocity of height growth. Young people reach that stage on average at age fifteen, but the committee noted that there is "much individual variation." Consequently, based on the contents of this article, the American Academy of Pediatrics recommends that each child's stage of physical maturity be assessed by medical personnel and that the adults who plan strength-training programs be qualified to develop programs appropriate for varying stages of maturity.

A February 2, 2006, note from the Mayo Clinic at their Web page, www.mayoclinic.com, also said: "Strength training for kids has gotten a bad reputation over the years.

Lifting weights, for example, was once thought to damage young growth plates—areas of cartilage that have not yet turned to bone. Experts now realize that with good technique and the right amount of resistance, young athletes can avoid growth plate injuries. Strengthening exercises, with proper training and supervision, provide many benefits to a young athlete."

What does this all mean? Knowledgeable trainers can help young athletes gain strength at all levels of play, and weight training will help them do so. If most kids are urged to do it, those who don't will be at a disadvantage. However, any program should avoid maximal weight lifts until the mid-high-school years.

Be careful; injury can still occur no matter what. Let's face it. Anyone who has ever lifted weights knows that even if a good program is followed, kids have a powerful urge to finish with some heavy weights to see how much they can lift. If unsupervised, they will go for the max at some point. This is one of the reasons I frown on the idea. I also resent the idea that we should heighten the competitive pressure of athletics in grade school by creating a need to strength train to "keep up." But the reality is that at the high-school level, players will need to lift weights if they are to be competitive. As a parent, you must ensure that they are supervised and that they follow a sound program. A 7 percent injury rate is quite high, so parents must assert control on this matter.

A player who undertakes a weight-training program, as advised above, should have the supervision and advice of a knowledgeable trainer. Parents should ask their doctors if any pre-existing health conditions would be aggravated by such training. High blood pressure is one condition that doesn't mix well with weights. Any pain should be reported to the trainer. Warm-up and stretching exercises should be done before lifting. Lifting maximal weights or engaging in ballistic, sudden jerking exercises, such as clean and jerk, should not be done. Kids should generally use weights in sets of fifteen repetitions. They should not lift every day, but every other day at the most. All major muscle groups should get some attention to keep development balanced.

In the weight room, baseball players should emphasize shoulder exercises and light leg exercises. Exercises using dumbbells for shoulder, wrist, and forearm strength, and for strengthening the rotator cuff are useful. My favorite exercise has the player lying on the bench with a dumbbell in each hand, arms extended outward, and elbows bent slightly. The player lifts the weights until they touch. It's the type of exercise that strengthens throwing ability. For the legs, work on hamstrings and knee strengthening. Let the trainer explain how to do these and other exercises needed for a balanced program.

VISION

The following will be the most important section in this book for some of your players, maybe for your own child. It reveals what may be the best-kept secret in baseball and perhaps in all of sports. It's all about eyesight: how critical it is and how to improve it. Good vision is perhaps more critical in baseball for hitting and fielding than in any other sport.

As I look back on my three decades of coaching baseball and at my success stories, I'm also reminded of the many young players who came to the game full of hope and excitement but who just never made it. Inexplicably, these players continually performed below the level I expected for them. Like all kids, they dreamed of those game-winning hits or rally-snuffing catches. They just never seemed to get it done.

Some of these kids were good athletes. They knew they could do better, knew they had it in them, but they could only put up average numbers. Some had a miserable season or two and never came back to the game.

Surely, for some it just wasn't there. Their gifts in life were elsewhere, in the laboratory, with music, or in other skills, just not in baseball. That's life. But I have become convinced that for many, a substantial part of the problem was merely in their inability to see the ball clearly enough to make solid contact or to judge accurately its distance and speed.

Stories about the importance of eyesight to baseball are legendary. Perhaps the most famous is that of Ted Williams, one of the best pure hitters of all time. He batted .344 lifetime, smacked 521 homers, won two Most Valuable Player awards and two triple crowns, and was the last player to hit over .400. Ted used to say that he could actually see the ball hit the bat. Well, we certainly teach our players to try to do that, but I've never seen a fastball hit my bat, and I doubt most people reading this book have either. The colorful, former umpire Ron Luciano challenged Ted on it one day. Ted smeared his bat with black pine tar and said he would hit the ball and then indicate whether the bat hit the seam on the ball or even whether it touched two seams. Williams got most of his answers right!

Ted mastered the rapid eye movements known as *saccades*, which relate to eye-tracking skills. When he was a kid, Ted used to hit bottle caps spun at him by a friend, and I believe this is what improved the rapid eye movements he needed to track a baseball.

Babe Ruth was found to have visual acuity far superior to the average player. Moreover, the importance of vision is clear from Major League's experience with the introduction of night baseball in the post-World War II era. The ball is harder to see at night; field lights don't equal normal daylight. The result is that the average batting average tumbled about twenty points. The difference between a .280 batting average and a .260 average will determine whether a player makes it or not in the pros. Just a small subtle difference in visual acuity is enough to lead to enormous differences in how well a batter can hit baseballs.

This fact is not lost on professional baseball players. Vision therapy is a rapidly growing part of the off-season preparation of Major League players. The sports literature reports that many other sports, such as golf, tennis, hockey, and basketball, also emphasize visual acuity in training routines.

The June 1992 issue of *Sport* magazine reported on Syd Thrift, then the Chicago Cubs assistant general manager and a long-time innovator in baseball, who introduced visual sensory training to his players. The article stated, "His eye training regimen consists of a series of vision tests, exercises for the fourteen eye muscles, and follow-up workouts designed to improve concentration, visual focus, depth perception, and hand-eye coordination." Thrift said, "Pitchers perform better since they are more focused on the target. Batters can use two eyes as one, picking up the ball as soon as it leaves the pitcher's hand and quickly identifying the pitch." The article noted that greats such as George Brett, Barry Bonds, and Bobby Bonilla benefited from the therapy, and that the best visual acuity tested had been Don Mattingly's.

In an astonishing book, *20/20 Is Not Enough: The New World of Vision*, Arthur S. Seiderman and Steven E. Marcus revealed new and effective ways to dramatically improve vision. They claimed that 70 percent of Americans have less than adequate vision. Moreover, vision is not fully developed until age ten or eleven. Intensive reading in school, watching television, and working at computer terminals all further reduce visual acuity. So, is it surprising that so many ten-year-olds in Little League don't make good contact with the ball? What is really frustrating is that the book suggests that most visual disorders go undiagnosed and could easily be treated.

The good news is that vision can be improved. Even if your child has 20/20 vision, this does not mean he cannot improve other aspects of vision such as depth perception, the ability to clearly track a fast-moving object, and hand-eye coordination. The difference with only a small amount of therapy can be enormous.

It is not the objective of this book to give medical advice or to go in depth on the biology of the eye itself. Another superb book that is available on this topic is: *Your Eyes!*, by Thomas L. D'Alonzo (Avanti Publishing, 1991).

The eyes are like binoculars, and when they don't work well together, they get out of focus. The result is difficulty in seeing things that are close (hyperopia or farsightedness), difficulty in seeing things far away (myopia or nearsightedness), difficulty judging depth or speed of an approaching object, or other ailments.

I advise you to visit an eye doctor to have your child's eyes tested. If one of your players seems to have some difficulty seeing the ball, let the parents know. Tell them to read this book, so they can consider whether it would be useful to engage in vision therapy even if there is a more obvious eye disorder.

Vision therapy has advanced far enough that some exercises can safely be done at home. I'll list a few that appear commonly in the literature and that apply to the skills needed in baseball. Again, if you think your child's eyesight is an issue, the best practice is first to seek a doctor's advice.

VISION-THERAPY DRILLS

1. Brock String. Tie a 4-foot string to an object at eye level while seated. Mark the center of the string and a point several inches from each end with a large knot or piece of black tape. Stretch the line taut and hold against the nose. Looking at the center spot will reveal an X pattern. (See figure 9-1 on page 145.) The far spot will reveal an A pattern, and the near spot shows a V pattern. Practice shifting the gaze from spot to spot until it feels smooth and easy to do. Eventually you can shorten the string. Do this for several minutes each day. It will improve focusing and depth perception. This drill can be done at home or at practice. (If done at home, ensure parental supervision. Exercises should not be overdone.)

2. Marsden Ball. Get a rubber ball about 4 inches in diameter. Write letters and numbers all over the ball in ink. (They should be clear, dark letters on a light-colored ball.) Suspend it overhead to about eye level while seated. Cover one eye and tap the ball lightly. Try to call out one of the letters you see and quickly touch it with your finger. Do each eye for a few minutes. This improves eye-hand coordination and the ability to track a moving object. If the ball can be affixed securely enough, use a broom handle to bounce it off a wall. Try to maintain a fluid and continuous pace. Use a smaller ball to make it tougher. Have one player hold the string for another.

3. Fixation Drill. Hang a ring on a string and suspend overhead to about eye level while standing. Stand a step away with a long pencil. Covering the left eye, step toward the ring with the right foot and, holding the pencil in the right hand, try to put the pencil through the ring without touching it. After a few minutes, switch eyes and use the left hand, stepping with the left foot. After mastering this drill, try it with a moving target. This drill improves hand-eye coordination.

143

4. Rotations. Place a marble in a pie tin or frying pan held about 15 to 18 inches from the eyes. Holding the head still, rotate the marble and try to follow it with the eyes for a few minutes. Change direction and repeat for another two minutes. This improves tracking ability.

5. Accommodation Drill. Doctors use a device called an Accomotrac, which is based on biofeedback theory, to improve focusing problems, particularly nearsightedness. An exercise you can do is with a newspaper of normal-sized print. Sit with the paper at just below eye level, as close as possible to the eye. Place a second newspaper with large headlines 15 to 20 feet away. Cover one eye. Shift focus back and forth from one newspaper to the other. This can also be done with any nearby small object and any distant object.

6. Convergence Drills. Place this book on a desk at normal reading distance, opened to show figure 9-2 (on page 145). Hold a pencil between the two sets of circles and slowly move the pencil point toward your eyes. At a point about 6 inches from your eyes, a third circle will appear between the other two. The outer circle should appear closer than the inner one. When it seems clear, shift the eyes to something else and bring them back again to the pencil tip. Do this until the focus remains smooth and clear upon the middle figure. Do it ten times.

Another convergence drill is to hold the circles up at reading distance but just below eye level. Sit several feet from a wall. Focus on the wall, and the third circle should again appear. This time, the small inner circle should appear closer. Close your eyes and reopen, focusing on the pencil point. Do this several times until the focus stays smooth and clear. After this is mastered, omit the pencil and move the figures a bit closer. You can also draw the figures on separate cards and separate them farther (just a bit, don't strain). Always try to get to a clear focus on the center set of circles.

Teach these drills to your players on rainy days. Tell them to do them at home. Some can be done at the field. Talk to parents about them so they can supervise these activities. Tell parents to get this book and read this section. Your team's vision will improve. Batting and fielding will improve. Hopefully, some of those kids who otherwise wouldn't make it will have some fun with this great game.

One final thought: Do you know which of your eyes is the dominant one is? Make a circle with your thumb and index finger, and extend your arm out at eye level. Fix your sight through the circle on a small object and close one eye, then open it and close the other. The dominant eye is the one for which the object does not move.

9-1. **VISION-THERAPY DRILLS**

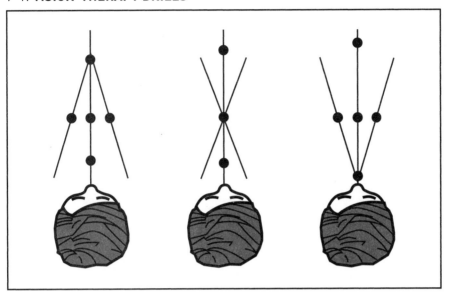

The Brock String vision-therapy drill improves focusing and depth perception. See the text for a detailed explanation of the drill.

9-2. **CONVERGENCE CIRCLES**

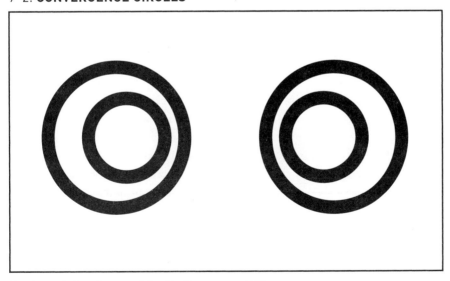

Use these circles when practicing the Convergence Drill.

Studies show that batters whose dominant eye is opposite their batting side (left eye for righty batters, right eye for lefties) hit for higher averages. The dominant eye is closer to the pitch.

INJURIES

Carefully check the practice fields. Are there stones or other protrusions? Are there any holes, ruts, or tracks? (This is how ankles get sprained.) If you see any, let the players know so they can avoid them. Perhaps you can get a few parents together to fill in any holes or remove any protrusions or other debris

Is there a trainer or someone qualified in first aid at practices? This is very important during the early days of the season. Most leagues require coaches to obtain licenses that expose them to first-aid techniques, but is there someone who really knows what to do? If not, remember that parents can take a course and become quite knowledgeable. Perhaps you can get a parent to volunteer as a trainer.

As a parent, it pays to attend a few practices to see how sensitive the coach is to injury. A good rule is that a player who complains of any injury to any joint cannot play for at least ten minutes to determine if pain or swelling is still present.

No matter how well-conditioned a team is, injuries can occur any time. A common injury is a groin strain, usually caused by sprinting down to first base without warming up. Strained knees, sprained ankles, sore thumbs on catching hands, and bruised ribs from getting hit by pitches are the most common injuries in baseball. Bloody noses, sprained wrists and forearms, jammed fingers, dislocations, and bruises also occur. Thankfully, broken bones are rare, but not rare enough. Most youth baseball teams don't have trained first-aid people, and they should. I went through the program for my son's team, and it was quite good. Remember that ambulances are not usually present at games or at practices where many injuries occur.

Abrasions often occur on the sides of the legs and elbows from sliding. These are the most likely cuts to get infected. Wash the wound as soon as possible, with soap if it is handy. Apply a dressing when you can—the sooner the better. Just put some antiseptic on it. See a physician if it gets red or filled with pus or if red tracks appear.

Lacerations are deeper wounds. Unless bleeding is severe, wash the wound and apply direct pressure with a bandage to stop the bleeding. If the wound is severe or deep, seek first aid. Keep applying pressure, and secure the dressing with a bandage (you can tie the knot right over the wound to reinforce the pressure). Immediately elevate the wound higher than the heart to help slow the bleeding. If the bandage over the wound gets blood-soaked, don't remove it—just apply a new dressing right over it. If the child has lost a lot of blood, you'll need to treat for shock. Keep the player warm with blankets and call for help. If a laceration is major, a butterfly bandage will hold the skin together. Consult a physician immediately for stitches.

Contusions and bruises occur frequently. Apply ice quickly after taking care of any abrasions or lacerations. Ice arrests internal bleeding and prevents or lessens swelling. Ice is the best first aid available for nearly any swelling from bruises or sprains. Apply it very quickly, within minutes, and much internal damage will be spared. Do not move the child, especially if he is down due to a hard collision. He could have a spinal injury, and the slightest movement by an untrained person could do serious damage.

Sprained ankles, knees, or wrists should be immobilized. Apply an ice pack immediately. Act as if there is a fracture until you're sure there is no fracture. Call the ambulance if there is any question. Get an X-ray to see if there is a break or other damage.

If there is a fracture, immobilize the child completely when possible. There should be no movement at all. Comfort him, keep him warm with coats or blankets, and get medical help. Do not allow your child to be moved or cared for by anyone who is not medically trained. If he is in the middle of the field during a championship game, the game can wait. Insist on this. Permanent damage can result from aggravating a break.

If a child ever falls to the ground unconscious, see if anyone present has been trained to handle this situation. The first move, once it is clear that the child will not respond, is to check for the vital signs, the ABCs of first aid: airway, breathing, and circulation. Send for an ambulance and let a trained person administer rescue breathing or CPR (cardiopulmonary resuscitation) as necessary. Try to stay calm and let the first responders do their job. In all my years of coaching four sports and playing even more, I've never seen CPR administered. I hope that you won't either.

Finally, heat exhaustion can occur during practices or games, particularly late in the season. A person with heat exhaustion feels clammy and pale. Remove the child from the playing field, apply cool towels, and elevate the feet. If the body temperature is very high and pupils are constricted, you should suspect heat stroke. Call an ambulance and cool him down fast. Treat for shock.

Knee injuries are tough. Often the injury will require some sort of arthroscopic surgery to mend cartilage. Modern procedures are quite advanced. Have the child see a knowledgeable sports doctor. Your high-school athletic director will know the name of one. Tell your child to play the game safely. Aggressiveness is okay, but players should never intentionally hurt someone. Hope that other parents give the

09

same advice. I play various sports frequently, and there are often one or two guys who take chances with the health of others. Don't encourage your child to grow up to be like them.

When an injury occurs, insist on rest. I've seen many kids rush back from a sprained ankle only to have the injury plague them through the years. Don't let it happen. Make sure that your child wears an ankle brace after recovery to prevent a repeat injury. There are excellent ankle braces on the market today. The point is that injuries need time to heal right. If you give them that time, the future can hold many years of sports for your child. If you don't, it could be over already.

SERIOUS INJURIES

Catastrophic spine or brain injuries among any athletes, especially baseball players, are rare. Yet they happen. I recall just a few years ago a teammate of mine who slid into second base. He dove head-first, but then turned his back into the second baseman. As his back hit the fielder's knee, he heard a crack. His back was broken; luckily, he recovered.

There are also cases where kids get hit in the head by a hit or thrown ball. This is a most unpleasant subject, but it is important that you understand some details.

Many deadly injuries of the brain, or paralyzing injuries of the spine, are caused by earlier blows, sometimes ones that occurred a week or more earlier. A concerned and informed parent can step in to prevent this. A player can receive a concussion and never black out, but the brain swelling can become lethal days later, triggered by a relatively minor blow.

Any level of confusion or headache brought on by a blow to the head should receive immediate medical attention. I don't care if it's a championship game—get the player out of the game! The Colorado Medical Society recommends that players who sustain a severe blow to the head be removed for at least twenty minutes and not allowed to return to the game if any confusion or amnesia persists during that time. A player who loses consciousness should go straight to the hospital.

THE CARBOHYDRATE DIET

Parents can do only so much to improve their child's athletic ability, but they can do a great deal to maintain his good health. All sports require a great deal of energy, and a healthy body goes a long way toward better performance on the field and avoiding injury.

Obviously, a balanced diet is essential. There are many books on diet, and your doctor or school nurse can provide the elements of good diet. Good nutrition helps develop strength, endurance, and concentration. A good diet balances proteins, carbohydrates, and fats. An athlete in training needs mainly complex carbohydrates to comprise about 70 percent of the total diet, with fats (10 percent) and proteins (20 percent) splitting the remainder. Popular today is the food guide pyramid. Complex carbohydrates dominate the base grouping, reflecting the greater servings of breads, cereal, rice, and pasta that are recommended. Vegetables and fruits take up the next level, calling for a few daily servings each. The dairy group and the meat, fish, and poultry group are next, with fats last.

Early in the season, an evening meal high in carbohydrates helps maintain energy for the next day. Pasta is the best meal for this. A banana each day during this early period helps prevent potassium depletion. Potassium facilitates the process of muscular contraction. Complex carbohydrates are the primary source of fuel and energy for the athlete. What is not needed is stored for future use. Avoid simple carbohydrates such as sugar and honey. The adage that a candy bar just before a game gives an energy boost is misleading since simple carbohydrates cause unstable supplies of glucose. (Ever notice how tired you feel after a sweets overload?) Good sources of complex carbohydrates are corn on the cob, wild rice, brown rice, whole wheat, and whole rye.

A TYPICAL HIGH-CARBOHYDRATE DIET

Breakfast
- 8 ounces orange juice or a grapefruit or 8 ounces apple juice
- Bowl of shredded wheat (low-fat milk) or oatmeal or cream of farina
- (a) Bacon and two eggs or (b) pancakes and butter
- Several slices of whole wheat toast and butter
- Daily vitamin
- 10 ounces water

Lunch
- 1 bowl of soup: chicken, clam chowder, or vegetable
- 2 pieces broiled chicken or 6 ounces broiled fish
- Green salad with oil and vinegar
- Cooked rice or a potato (no French fries)
- 2 slices of enriched bread
- 12 to 16 ounces milk
- 10 ounces water

Dinner
- 1 bowl of soup: cream of mushroom, cream of potato, or vegetable
- Linguine with tomato or clam sauce
- Baked potato
- Cooked vegetable: corn, broccoli, peas, or beans
- Beverage of choice
- 10 ounces water

Desserts or Snacks
- Bananas, apples, raisins, strawberries, or melons
- 10 ounces water

Because children have special fluid needs, fluids play a critical role in maintaining health and performance of the child athlete. Heat stroke ranks second among reported causes of death in high-school athletes. All teams should allow water breaks, so make sure parents know to get their children water bottles. Mid-practice is not a good time to load up on too much water, so tell the kids to limit themselves to a cup at each break. Kids need a couple of quarts a day, or more if it's hot and they are playing outside. Drinking plenty of water is a good habit, so be sure they know to drink some at each meal. It is also important to drink plenty of fluids before, during, and after practices. Dehydration reduces performance and can lead to serious medical problems.

Sufficient sleep is also a concern. If your son starts the season with tough practice sessions, you won't have to worry too much, since he will come right home and hit the pillow. However, into the season, particularly at high-school levels, a player may try to burn the candle at both ends. I find that kids relate better to my advice when they consider the practical consequences of their actions. Lack of sufficient rest diminishes performance. Diminished performance costs playing time.

COACHES' AND PARENTS' CHECKLISTS 10

Now that you have read the book, it's time to get outside and have some fun with your team. I find it useful when I coach to have a checklist of things to remember during practice. For instance, when a kid is batting at practice, I glance at the checklist and it reminds me to focus on different parts of the swing. It also reminds me to keep repeating several things, like "Keep your hands up," "Open your hips with power as you make contact," and "Look at the ball." So here is a checklist for you to use.

HITTING

1. Keep your eye on the ball as it moves from the pitcher's hand to the bat. See the whole ball. Watch it spin.

2. Practice the proper stance.
   - ☐ Feet under or just outside of the shoulders.
   - ☐ Stand as deep as allowed in the batter's box.
   - ☐ Rear foot should be back a bit—farther from the plate than the front foot.
   - ☐ Weight a bit forward, toward plate, on balls of toes, a bit more on rear foot. Feel balanced in the legs.
   - ☐ Bend knees a bit, enough to feel loose.
   - ☐ Bend waist forward a bit.
   - ☐ Hands together, an inch from the end of the bat. Use a light bat.
   - ☐ Grip bat firmly, but don't squeeze it; "feel" strength in the wrists.
   - ☐ Hands up, even with, and slightly behind, the rear shoulder, about 6 inches out.
   - ☐ Bat points up and back a bit toward the catcher.
   - ☐ Back elbow up, at least a bit, away from body, shoulders level (or front shoulder down a bit).

151

☐ Chin tucked close to front shoulder, front shoulder tucked toward plate and down a bit. Head faces the pitcher.

☐ Be still. No dancing, no wiggling bat, and no wiggling the hips. Still, but not stiff.

3. Swing properly.

☐ Cock and load. Rotate very slightly away from the pitch and gather power.

☐ Get a good pitch in the strike zone. See the ball immediately in front of you.

☐ Stride into the pitch, toward the pitcher, while driving ("squashing the bug") off the back toe-pad.

☐ Thrust then open the hips, then the shoulders. Swing level, almost coming down on the ball, never uppercut. Keep head and front shoulder down. Move hands directly at the ball.

☐ Don't hitch or wind up and cock the bat at the beginning of the swing. Hands are still, and the only movement is to thrust hands directly to the ball.

☐ Extend the arms, whipping the head of the bat through the ball.

☐ Hit through the ball and follow through.

4. Use good bunting form.

☐ Turn and face the pitcher squarely, or at least open the hips, as he releases the ball.

☐ Slide top hand along the bat about one-third to one-half the distance, cradling the bat head between the thumb and next finger. The left hand can travel toward the middle also, if it helps bat control and does not undermine grip.

☐ Keep the head of the bat high, coming down to the ball. Concentrate on the ball.

☐ Let the ball hit the bat, guiding the ball down the third base line.

☐ Spring from the batter's box immediately upon contact.

☐ Don't look at the ball, just run like the dickens.

FIELDING

1. Catching

☐ Quickly get under pop-ups. Catch the ball above the head, fingers up, palms out, in the web of the glove. Use both hands. Err on the side of being too deep; it's easier to run in than it is to backpedal. If you must go back, turn and run instead of running backwards. Use a rubber ball at first.

152

☐ Get in front of grounders. Step to the ball, spread legs, get glove down, bend knees, body low, weight forward. Scoop ball into gut, hands soft. Challenge ball affirmatively. Don't come up too soon, and keep the head down.

2. Throwing

☐ Push off with same foot as throwing arm.

☐ Get set and balanced.

☐ Point front foot and shoulder at target.

☐ Reach back and extend arm with throw.

☐ Grip ball with two fingers on top. Ball shouldn't be too far back in palm.

☐ Look at target's glove. Don't aim, and throw as level as possible. Throw hard unless target is close, then throw underhand. Crow hop.

☐ Throw ahead of the lead runner to the cutoff.

3. Rundowns

☐ Get the runner to commit first.

☐ Run the runner back to the prior base.

☐ Hold ball high, faking a throw.

☐ Receiving fielder stands on field side of base, a step in front of the base. Tag low.

☐ Other fielders must back up the fielders in the rundown.

RUNNING AND SLIDING

1. Running Bases

☐ Sprint to all bases. Hook pattern to first base.

☐ Run on the balls of the toes, head and shoulders forward, arms churning.

☐ Know where the ball is at all times; always try to anticipate the chance to advance to the next base.

☐ Run through the bag.

☐ Plant left foot on the inside of the base and lean into the turn (either foot is okay).

☐ Expect to take another base.

☐ Try to draw the throw; fake advancing to next base; make things happen; get people's attention.

☐ Go halfway to next the base on a fly ball.

153

2. Sliding

    ☐ Lift arms up, right leg tucked in under left.

    ☐ Slide flat on the butt, avoid turning on side. Stay low, flat.

    ☐ Don't break the fall with the hands.

    ☐ Slide away from the ball.

BASEBALL POSITIONS

1. Catcher

    ☐ Crouch, on toes, squatting, not on one knee.

    ☐ Don't get too far back from the plate.

    ☐ Let the ball come to the glove, fingers up if high, down if low, hands soft.

    ☐ Catch one-handed. Keep free hand behind the back, fist clenched.

    ☐ Control the pitcher, slow him down, keep him loose and strong, and focus him on your glove.

    ☐ Look for fielders out of position.

    ☐ Block pitches in the dirt.

    ☐ Practice "quickness" on steals—retrieve ball, snatch and fire in one motion.

    ☐ Tag at plate low, block plate, mask off, using two hands.

    ☐ Practice foul tips, bunts, and pop-ups. Practice snatch and lob.

2. First Baseman

    ☐ Get to bag quickly, touch bag with foot opposite glove hand.

    ☐ Don't stretch for the ball until you see the path of the throw, then stretch to meet it.

    ☐ Go get bad throws, leaving the base if necessary.

    ☐ Play the hop. Practice throws in the dirt (wear catcher's gear if available).

    ☐ Go for all grounders. Lob to pitcher, show him the ball, lead him slightly.

    ☐ Know your area. Practice foul pop-ups.

    ☐ Hold the runner.

    ☐ Once the runner has second base, move into the infield area to help out.

3. Second Baseman

    ☐ Knock grounders down.

    ☐ Stance: Stay low, weight forward, eye on the ball to the hands, stay under the ball, and scoop it out in front.

    ☐ Know where you are going to throw the ball.

☐ Get all pop-ups to the right side.

☐ Cutoff on outfield balls to right side.

☐ Pivot man on double plays.

☐ Primary receiver on infield pop-up to right side.

☐ Cover first base on bunts to right side.

4. Shortstop

☐ Play deep in the hole.

☐ Stance: Stay low, weight forward, eye on the ball to the hands, stay under the ball, and scoop it out in front.

☐ Practice quick transition from catch to throw.

☐ Cutoff for left side of outfield or on any play to third base.

☐ Primary receiver on infield pop-ups; can call off anyone.

☐ Hold runners on third base on grounders before throwing to first base.

☐ Straddle the bag low on tags, especially steals, glove down.

5. Third Baseman

☐ Know where the fence is.

☐ Play in close. Dive when needed.

☐ Need to make plays on steal; must primarily stop the ball, then tag low.

6. Outfield

☐ Most action is to the right side; right fielder needs to have strongest arm.

☐ Get under the ball. Start laterally then get to where it will land. Charge a ground ball. Block outfield grounders, lowering body to one knee.

☐ Know where to throw ahead of time. Know where the lead runner is.

☐ Catch with hands high, palm outward, two hands. Don't hold the ball; throw immediately to the cutoff.

☐ Turn and run if ball is over the head.

☐ Back up bases on steals.

7. Pitcher

☐ Don't practice too much; arm will burn out. Be sure to get rest.

☐ Start from same spot and position. Consistency is key.

☐ Grip ball with fingers, crossing the seams, ball away from palm. Address batter, hands at side, take a breath.

☐ Rock the body and begin the windup. Pivot.

155

- ☐ Crane. Lift front knee straight up, looking at strike zone.
- ☐ Reach straight back with ball.
- ☐ Stride and drive. Rock forward, kick front leg out toward batter, drive hard with back leg, lunging toward the batter.
- ☐ Stay closed. Until the stride foot lands, keep the door closed.
- ☐ Point and plant front foot, and explosively open the door. Whip open the left shoulder, extend the throwing arm, keep elbow up, snap wrist, and throw over the top. Open up hips and come down flat but hard, with front foot in same place every time. Follow through gracefully. These are separate moves, but all flow together.
- ☐ Consistency, gracefulness, smoothness, confidence are keys.
- ☐ Take your time, don't rush in between pitches, get into a rhythm.
- ☐ Know your batters, challenge them, throw strikes.
- ☐ Cover first base on grounders to the first base side.
- ☐ Come home on wild pitches or passed balls.
- ☐ Pitch from the stretch with runners on.

GLOSSARY

As with all sports, baseball has its own language and jargon. Here are some terms so you can "talk baseball" as well as anyone.

Ace: A team's best starting pitcher.

Appeal: A fielder may raise a claim and request the umpire's judgment when: a runner leaves a base too soon; does not tag up on a fly ball; misses a base when running; or a batter checks a swing, but the bat still gets through the strike zone. If the umpire saw it, he will make the appropriate call—out, strike, return to base, etc.

Around the horn: A double play starting with the third baseman, a throw to second base, and then on to first base.

Backstop: The fence that partially encloses the batter's box from behind. It is usually tall enough to keep foul tips from going too far back and out of the playing area.

Balk: I've never seen this called in Little League play, but it's in the rulebook. A balk is a penalty for a pitcher faking a pitch to get a base runner off-balance. Since there is no stealing until the ball reaches the batter (except in "50–70" games), the main thing a balk is supposed to eliminate can't happen anyway. If the pitcher is on the rubber and makes any motion indicating the beginning of the pitch, or feigns a throw to a base, the runners are all allowed to advance one base. It is also a balk if the pitcher does not come to a complete stop between his windup and the pitch. In 1988 umpires started calling this in the Major Leagues and it led to a period of much confusion.

Ball: A pitch outside of the strike zone. Four balls in a single at bat entitle the batter to go to first base, called a *walk*.

Base bag: There are three of them, one at each corner of the infield. While on base, the runner can't be tagged out, unless he was forced to advance. The fourth base is called *home plate*.

Baselines: The white chalk lines that extend from home plate through first and third base to the outfield foul poles. These lines divide fair and foul territory.

Batter's box: A 3-foot by 6-foot box on either side of the plate, starting 27½ inches behind the back top of the plate, and coming up 4 inches from the side of the plate. The batter must be entirely inside the box when hitting the ball.

Batting average: Number of hits divided by number of at bats. It's a good measure of hitting ability. In professional baseball, an average over .300 is very good. This measure is not heavily used in youth ball due to the difficulty of determining errors.

Batting order: The sequence in which kids take turns batting. First up is the *lead-off* batter; the fourth batter is the *clean-up*. Normally, the first two batters are good hitters who will also take a walk if available. Their job is to get on base. Positions three, four, and five are power hitters, looking to drive in runners on base. The slots from six to nine are usually for hitters with lower batting averages.

Breaking ball: A pitch that carries a lot of spin, designed to make the ball curve or break direction as it travels toward the batter, making it necessary for the batter to adjust his swing accordingly. The ball breaks because the spin creates greater pressure on the part of the ball that spins forward. On a fastball, the bottom of the ball spins forward, so the ball rises. I rarely hear of kids being taught to throw a curve, slider, knuckleball, sinker, hook, or other breaking pitch. A kid can hurt his arm snapping his wrist if he does it wrong. The rules don't prohibit it, but I've seen umpires tell the kid to stop.

Bullpen: A separate section in foul territory where the professional pitchers sit in the big leagues. It's where they warm up in case they get called in.

Catch: We all know what a catch is, but the rule is that you have to possess a ball long enough to prove complete control of the ball. If you catch it squarely and then fall and dislodge the ball, it's not a catch. Different kinds of catches include basket, over the shoulder, diving, and backhand. A catch is also called a *stab* and a *grab*. A ball that bounces just as a player catches it is called a *trap*. One that bounces just before a player catches it is a *short-hop*. A *can of corn* is a soft pop-up that was easy to catch.

Caught looking: A batter who strikes out on a called third strike; that is, he does not swing at it.

Checked swing: A swing stopped after going about halfway. If the bat crosses the plate, it is a strike.

Choke up: Holding the hands farther up the handle of the bat, a few inches closer to the fat end. It makes the bat lighter and easier to control. Smaller players or players with two strikes should always choke up. Bat speed is important. It does, however, reduce power.

Clean-up: The fourth batter in the batting order, who is usually adept at driving home (cleaning up) any runners on base.

Count: The number of balls and strikes on a batter during one at bat.

Crane: The movement made by a pitcher as he lifts his foot high in the air when he is about to pitch. It looks like a crane lifting its leg.

Dead ball: A ball out of play; play is suspended. Examples include a batter hit by a pitch, a runner hit by a batted ball, a ball that goes into the dugout or any other out-of-bounds area.

Diamond: A name given to the infield, outlined by the four basepaths and roughly resembling a diamond.

Double play: When the defense gets two outs during one play. A double play usually occurs when a runner is on first, and an infielder touches second and throws to another fielder who touches first base with the ball before the runner gets there. The play at each base is called a *force play*. Another double play situation often occurs when a fly ball is caught and the ball is thrown to a base before a runner can get back to tag up.

Dugout: The place where players sit while waiting to play. Usually, in the big leagues, it's an area with a bench, dug a few feet into the ground (where it's cooler).

Error: The failure of a fielder to catch a ball that should have been caught with ordinary effort, or an errant throw resulting in prolonging the at bat or a runner's advance. Mistakes or slowness are not errors. An error is also called a *boot*, a *muff*, or *throwing the ball away*.

Follow through: In hitting or pitching, allowing the bat or the pitcher's hand to continue along its normal course after the hit or pitch occurs. It allows for more control and power in both activities.

Force play: When a runner must advance on a batted ball because all bases behind him are filled with runners. For instance, if bases are loaded, everyone must reach the next base. If there are runners on first and second, both must advance to make room on first for the batter. A runner on first must get to second to make room for the batter. The forced runner is out if a fielder with the ball touches a base that the runner must advance to before the runner gets there.

Foul: A *foul ball* is a batted ball that lands in foul territory. The *foul territory* is the area outside of the two foul lines. The *foul lines* run along the first and third baselines and extend out to the boundaries of the field, usually a fence. If the bat just tips the ball and it still goes to the catcher, it's called a *foul tip.*

Fungo: An extra-thick bat used for hitting grounders or fly balls for defensive practice. It makes it easier to hit the ball. (Remember, I recommend just throwing the ball for accuracy. It's tough to hit a fungo bat consistently for accuracy.)

Gap: The area in the outfield between outfielders, also called the *alley.*

Gamer: A kid who really hustles and likes the game. Also, a game-winning hit.

Grand slam: A home run hit when there is a runner on each base; four runs are scored.

Green light: A sign from the coach that allows a batter to swing at the next pitch. This is often an issue when the count is three balls and no strikes. In this case, a coach usually wants the batter to take a pitch (to not swing) and perhaps gain a walk. But a very good batter may be given the "green light" since the pitcher will try to make a good pitch.

Grounder: A ball that hits and travels or bounces along the ground in the infield.

Ground-rule double: A ball that bounces over the outfield fence or is touched by a fan after bouncing in fair territory. The batter advances to second base.

Heat: A good fastball. "Bring some heat" is a call to throw a bit harder.

Hit: When a batter safely advances at least to first base on a batted ball that lands in fair territory. Hits can be *singles*, *doubles*, *triples*, or *home runs*. A home run with bases loaded (runners on each base) is a *grand slam*. A *pop-up* or *fly ball* is hit high up into the air. If it drops between the outfield and infield (shallow outfield), it is a *bloop* or a *Texas-leaguer*. Hitting the ball is also called *sticking it, poking it, rapping it,* or *nailing it*. A *line drive* is the most desirable hit, also called a *rope*.

Hit and run: A signal from the coach for a runner to run and a batter to swing with the next pitch. Does not occur much in youth ball.

Inning: The professional baseball game is divided into nine innings. Youth baseball teams usually play six or seven innings. An inning is played when each team has had a chance to bat. Once each team has made three outs in its half-inning, a new inning starts. If the score is tied after nine innings, the game continues until an inning ends with one team ahead.

Interference: Running into or obstructing a fielder trying to make a play; moving in a manner to hinder or distract a batter. In the first instance, the runner is out and other runners return to the last base they touched. The ball is dead. In the second situation, the umpire warns the fielder to stop. If a fielder interferes with a runner, it is called *obstruction*.

Lead: When a runner takes a few steps toward the next base before the ball is pitched. This is not allowed in Little League play on smaller fields for ages twelve and under. You cannot leave the base until the ball has reached the batter. Some leagues allow it for twelve year olds, and for some eleven-year-old All-Star teams.

Lead-off: The first batter in the line up. Also the first batter in any inning.

Line drive: A hard hit ball in the air, but that is hit in a straight line as opposed to a pop-up.

Mound: Small hill that the pitcher stands on when pitching.

Obstruction: A fielder blocking the basepath. Baserunners should be given free access to run from base to base without being physically blocked or hindered by a fielder. If obstructed, the runner is awarded the base he would have advanced to according to the umpire's judgement. A fielder need not move from the path of a baserunner if he is in the act of fielding or is in possession of the ball.

On deck: The batter who is up next during his team's time at bat. He stands in a small circle in foul territory and warms up, usually with a heavily weighted bat.

Passed ball: A pitch missed by the catcher that should have been caught, as opposed to a wild pitch which could not be caught. There are many of both types in youth baseball.

Pinch runner: A runner who comes into the game to run for another player. This occurs in many leagues for pitchers and catchers at two outs, allowing both to get ready for the next inning.

Pitch: A thrown ball from the pitcher to the batter that begins baseball play. A hard, straight pitch is a *fastball*. Another pitch is a *change-up*, or a *change of pace*, when the ball is thrown slowly after a normal windup. A ball thrown at a batter is a *beanball* or a *dust-off pitch*. At advanced levels, such pitching tactics are encouraged to make a batter worried or distracted. A pitch that can't be caught is a *wild pitch*; it if can be caught but isn't, the catcher is charged with a *passed ball*. If the pitcher wets the ball, causing the ball to move erratically, it is illegal, and is called a *spitball*. Another illegal way to get a ball to move is to scuff up part of it so that the scuff catches air as the ball spins. The *knuckleball* or *screwball* is a pitch that can break several times or in any direction.

Putout: A play resulting in an out by striking a batter out, catching a fly ball, tagging a runner with the ball, or forcing a runner out.

Scoring position: A runner on second or third base is said to be in scoring position since a base hit will usually allow him to score.

Steal: When a runner advances to the next base on his own, without a hit or walk. This occurs often when the ball gets past the catcher.

Strike zone: The area over home plate from the batter's knees to his armpits, when the batter is in his normal batting stance. If any part of a pitched ball passes through this area, the batter is charged with a strike. Three strikes are an *out*. Strike zones often vary by umpires; this is the source of most arguments in baseball.

Tag: Touching a runner not on base with the ball or with a glove containing the ball.

Umpires: Umpires stand behind home plate and call the pitches strikes or balls. They are also in charge of calling fair and foul balls and determining whether or not baserunners are safe or out. Umpire signals are shown in the illustrations on page 163.

UMPIRE SIGNALS

INDEX